# ON LIFE
# AND LIVING

# ON LIFE
# AND LIVING

## Konrad Lorenz

IN CONVERSATION WITH
KURT MÜNDL
TRANSLATED BY RICHARD
D. BOSLEY

St. Martin's Press   New York

*Grateful acknowledgment is made for permission to reproduce the following photographs:* frontispiece, *Votava* /Vienna; part one, Günther Nenning/ Vienna; part two, *Paris Match* /Paris; part three, *Votava* /Vienna; part four, *Votava* /Vienna.

Library of Congress Cataloging-in-Publication Data

Lorenz, Konrad.
    [Rettet die Hoffnung. English]
    On life and living : Konrad Lorenz in conversation with Kurt Mündl.
      p. cm.
    Translation of: Rettet die Hoffnung.
    ISBN 0-312-03901-8
    1. Lorenz, Konrad—interviews.  2. Ethologists—Austria—Interviews.  I. Mündl, Kurt L.  II. Title.
QL31.L76A3  1990                       89-24118
591'.092—dc20                              CIP

First published in Austria by Jugend and Volk Verlagsges.m.b.H. under the title *Rettet die Hoffnung.*

First U.S. Edition
10 9 8 7 6 5 4 3 2 1

# CONTENTS

# INTRODUCTION
# HOW IT ALL HAPPENED

*O*ctober 1978 was a rainy month. On one of these rainy days, my friend Robert Czeck appeared at my door with his delivery truck, saying, "Come with me to Professor Lorenz's!" Czeck, who sold animals, was a steady supplier of Konrad Lorenz, furnishing him regularly with coral fish.

Since from my earliest years I had devoured everything that came from the pen of Konrad Lorenz, it was almost incomprehensible to me that I would become personally acquainted with my idol in this roundabout way. Less than two hours later, I actually stood—I confess, weak in the knees—before this world-famous man with snow-white hair and beard. My heart began to beat at its normal rhythm again after he greeted me in his extremely friendly way. I was directed to the best seat in front of the large aquarium.

Like a child enraptured by a gift for which he had longed, Konrad Lorenz began spontaneously and hastily to free the fish from their plastic bags as quickly as possible. He put these new subjects for study into the 32,000-liter aquarium. Visibly pleased with this addition to his collection, he sank with relish into his old leather chair and began a passionate conversation about coral fish. After a while he asked me, "Are you also interested in ocean fish?" I replied that my "specialty" was Ranidae (frogs) and Colubridae (adders), and that even as a preschool child I had kept a fire salamander as a pet. Konrad Lorenz laughed and slapped his knee breeches. He said, "That's a funny coincidence. My first animal was a fire salamander, too." That provided the basis for a lively discussion. Hours passed in a wink, and the Nobel Prize winner said as I left, "I hope that I have seriously infected you with my ideas; if you need anything, just come by and see me."

This "infection" was indeed so serious that only two weeks later I was again a guest in the Lorenz's house. On this next occasion, between a marvelous *Beuschel*—an Austrian dish made of calf's lungs—and an equally delicious pudding for dessert, I told him about my wild scheme of writing a book with photographs and text about our native forest. Konrad Lorenz did not dismiss my project as mad; after all, I was only nineteen then. On the contrary, he promised, after examining my work, to write an introduction for it. My happiness was complete when he said to his wife: "Imagine, my young friend has the marvelous idea of writing a book about the forest."

At the time, I couldn't imagine that this would not be his only introduction for a book of mine: Konrad Lorenz, in fact, supported my career as a science journalist many, many times in the most unselfish manner. He not only wrote prefaces but personally introduced the films I later made for television, and was always available for an interview.

Now ten years have passed. During this time, I spent unforgettable hours, afternoons, and evenings in Lorenz's house, garden, and in the aquarium room. My tape recorder was my constant companion during all of these years when I went to see Lorenz, since I had the honor of being allowed to visit him several times a year, not only for purely professional reasons but also socially. Our discussions were worthy of the name and had nothing in common with the usual question-and-answer style of the journalist and interviewee; and so I gathered a precious collection on the most diverse topics.

The year 1988 was not only the year in which Konrad Lorenz celebrated his eighty-fifth birthday but was also an anniversary for me, namely ten years of conversing with the man to whom I owe so much.

For that reason, I felt it my duty to transform these conversations into a book so that others could partake of the complex thoughts of Konrad Lorenz, the man and scholar, who, despite all his criticism of man's actions today, has never abandoned his faith in man.

KURT MÜNDL
Kirchstetten, Austria
August 15, 1988

# PART ONE

# Excerpts from the Life of a Natural Scientist

*"If I had not had
personal contact
with wild
animals during
my earliest
childhood, I
might have
become an
engineer."*

# LORENZ ON LORENZ

*M**uch has been written about you. How would you describe your career in your own words?*

It all began when my parents thought that I was a myoma. After all, my mother was over forty. I was by no means an accident; on the contrary, my parents wanted me very much, but they were so surprised by my conception that they couldn't believe it at first.

As I said, first phase: myoma. Then I grew so fast that people thought I was malignant. Oddly enough, that was Dr. Chrobak's diagnosis—Chrobak, the famous obstetrician who served the Austrian imperial house. My father, who was a doctor himself, an orthopedist, was more concerned about what was growing in my mother's uterus than other fathers might have been. As a result, he sent my mother to the famous Chrobak, who declared that I was a myoma. When my mother returned to Chrobak several weeks later with the real diagnosis, it was turned into a joke. The famous obstetrician said, "My, my, madam, who would have imagined such a thing?" My mother, prepared to respond in kind, answered, "A famous obstetrician, for example, might have thought of it. . . ."

My father, however, could not be calmed so easily. He was by no means certain that a child of such relatively old parents could really be all right. But, well, I did receive Immanuel Kant's chair in Königsberg and the Nobel Prize, and that is something.

My brother, Adolf, was eighteen years old when I was born, and there is a very funny picture of me standing on a table next to him. I had just learned to stand, so the picture was entitled "The two one-year olds." I was just one year old and my brother wore the uniform of a first-year cadet. My life throughout has been marked by a great deal of good fortune. First of all, it was very good fortune that I grew up in the countryside, in a house with a large garden, with very tolerant parents who gave me a good deal of liberty. Moreover, I became familiar with animals at a very early age.

As you know, children pretend to be things. They pretend that they are ducks, rabbits, engineers, and so on. Most children pretend that they are engineers. However, I first pretended to be an owl. I wanted to be an owl because they don't have to go to sleep at night. In our family, the large Caucasian walnut tree in front of the house is still called an "owl tree" because I played owl in it. The Caucasian walnut is an unusually good tree for climbing when it is still short, because many of its branches grow horizontally. The trunk in front was mine, while the one in back, which was harder to climb, belonged to the girl whom I later married. This was because she was older than I and could climb better.

In short, the owl was my ideal. Then I learned to swim and came into contact with water in other ways: I received a spotted salamander that was going to breed. Spotted salamander larvae were the first animals that I had for an aquarium. I was critical of the owl for not being able to swim, and exactly at this time, I became deeply impressed by a book: Selma Lagerlöf's *Nils Holgersson's Wonderful Trip.** It is a curious coincidence that this was also the first book that deeply impressed my friend Karl Popper. However, he once commented during a television broadcast that whereas he fell in love with Selma Lagerlöf after reading the book, Konrad Lorenz fell in love with the wild geese!

With such an influence, I wanted to be a wild goose. I pretended to be a goose and a duck, and since pretending to be something and to own something become mixed in children, I at least wanted to own a goose. However, my mother wouldn't agree, since a goose would do too much damage to the garden, and so I had to be content with a duckling. My father, however, was against that, maintaining that a five-year-old would only kill the duckling with too much attention. There was, however, a woman who looked after me named Resi Führinger. She was the daughter of wealthy farmers, a sort of patrician family of farmers, from southern Austria, who sent their daughters to be parlor maids in Vienna to complete their upbringing. Resi had a "green thumb" for raising animals. She cared for the larvae of the spotted salamander—I won't claim that I was the one who did it—and at least they lived. The duckling also lived.

As though it were yesterday, I remember having a bad conscience when I understood that the duckling was "crying." The duckling had cried "peep peep peep." I knew how the mother duck gave orders to the ducklings (not bad for a five-year-old) and I said "oarrk puu puu puu oarrk oarrk oarrk puu puu puu" with a tone of leadership. I remember that the duckling stopped crying, and instead of making a "peep peep peep" sound, it went "pipipp pipipp pipipp," its normal talking noise, and then it followed me. That was actually my first experience of influencing something. I cannot forget these experiences of my early childhood.

When people say, with good reason, that my most important

*Trans. note: a Swedish children's book not translated into English.*

contribution to the world is the theory of evolutionary episte-mology, I must then add that the fact that I was always convinced that I was related to animals played a role. I believe that an animal is a living being like myself, no better and no worse. I believed that the duckling was crying and I tried to comfort it.

This fundamentally simple attitude toward man—toward nature—is perhaps the most important thing I learned during my childhood. However, the story continues. I loved ducks, owned various ducks, and was interested in different types of ducks. I had an aquarium and bred fish. Whenever I can, I now advocate the aquarium as a pedagogic device. We have decided, in fact, not to give the next Konrad Lorenz Prize to an individual but to use the money to provide many children with aquariums. After a year, we'll give a prize to the child who has the best aquarium. It's an ingenious idea, which suits me well, since the aquarium helped form my personality. An aquarium teaches children ecology: It is a closed system in vitro that can collapse. In his formative years, a child can learn about over-population: One simply cannot go on adding one fish after another without the system suddenly collapsing.

Therefore, I came to know much about fish, fish that are similar and other fish, live bearers and cichlids, that are very different. I also learned about different varieties of ducks. I really wanted to study paleontology, which brings me to another story: I was sitting under the Caucasian walnut tree eating bread and honey. My mother was afraid of a wasp and wanted to shoo it away. However, my father didn't permit her to, and he showed me the wasp's abdomen, the respirating abdomen with the sections that fit into one another like a telescope. He told me that the wasp is an insect and that it is composed of metameres that move beautifully as they breathe. He showed me how beautiful a wasp is, that it's not at all ugly or horrid. That impressed me so much that even today I remember exactly where that happened—it's curious that at such times one remembers exactly where the event took place—at the table under the Caucasian walnut tree.

Not long thereafter, I found a rain worm, which expanded and contracted its segments like a telescope as it wriggled. I asked my father whether a rain worm was also an insect, but he didn't know. Even though he was a doctor, he couldn't give me a clear answer. A little later, I came across a book by Wilhelm Bölsche, *Die Schöpfungstage*.* It had a picture of the archaeopteryx, the earliest bird, which still had teeth in its jawbones, a long lizard's tail, and only a few feathers stuck in each wing. It was clear to me—I must have been a very clever child—that the rain worm is to the wasp as the archaeopteryx is to the bird of today! I swear that I am not imagining it!

I know I was still very young at the time because Resi had to read Bölsche's book aloud to me. By the age of six or seven, I could read well, so it must have been before then. Today I can still draw the pictures in Bölsche's book from memory. In the book, there was an anglicus, a prehistoric crab. I remember perfectly that Resi couldn't pronounce Latin names. There was also a picture of iguanodons, iguanodons sinking into the mud flats. I am absolutely certain that Resi read aloud, because she said "igonaunodons," and my wife and I, who were then just neighbors, played at being "igonaunodons." We stuck sections of an old garden hose into the waistbands of our trousers so that we would have tails trailing behind us, and we held our thumbs up—you know that iguanodons have a spike on each thumb, which they use as a weapon—and paraded proudly as "igonaunodons" through the garden!

It was at this time that I began to understand the importance of the development of a species, of phylogeny, of evolution. I was so influenced by Bölsche's book that I wanted to become a paleontologist. I thought that paleontology, the study of fossils—plants and animals that have turned to stone—was most interesting. I understood perfectly that phylogeny and evolution were the mysteries of the world, and I recall that

*Trans. note: One part of this book was published in English under the title* The Evolution of Man.

while taking a walk on the Vorderberg I told my father about everything that Resi had read to me. I babbled and talked a lot as a child, so my father often said with a pleading voice, "Pipe down for a moment!" During this one walk, I recall he didn't say anything, but just listened to me. While I explained the whole theory of evolution to him, he smiled approvingly and listened attentively. Suddenly, I understood that he already knew it all! Upon realizing this, I became extremely angry with my father because he understood something so important and hadn't thought it was worth the trouble to tell me.

As a result of these childhood experiences, I sincerely desired to study paleontology. My father was against it, however, and wanted me to study medicine. Since I was a good, obedient son, that's what I did. It wasn't really so bad, since I immediately encountered Ferdinand Hochstetter, who taught systematic anatomy. Hochstetter not only taught anatomy but also comparative anatomy and especially comparative embryology. Hochstetter had the gift of being able to teach clearly and methodically, to reconstruct the phylogeny of living animals from their similarities and dissimilarities. I can still hear Hochstetter saying, "Don't say 'a primitive animal.' There are no primitive animals, only primitive traits." Even the tuatara is a modern animal. Wonderful!

I like to say that I really would have had to be much more stupid than I was at eighteen and nineteen *not* to have seen that the methods that Hochstetter had worked out and taught about morphology could have been transferred without any changes to the behavior of ducks and cichlids. Thus occurred the birth of comparative behavioralism. That same year, I became acquainted with the man who discovered my discovery, Oskar Heinroth, who also studied the history of comparative development and who was the author of the revolutionary book *Die Vögel Mitteleuropas.* * Years later, we discovered an American named Charles Wittman who had written about the same ideas

*Trans. note: The title translates as* The Birds of Middle Europe. *The book was not translated into English.*

in 1899, ten years before Heinroth. Heinroth wrote his book in 1914 and I wrote mine in 1923.

I had, therefore, the opportunity to study comparative behavioralism. I became an assistant professor of comparative psychology, and neglected anatomy to write my postdoctoral dissertation *(Habilitationsschrift)*. At that time, it wasn't common to be an assistant professor in two different fields; after all, psychology was a subject in the humanities department. Another stroke of luck followed. The first stroke of luck had been Resi, the second Bölsche and Hochstetter, and the third was the teaching position in Königsberg. This position in Königsberg was actually first given to Eduard Baumgarten, a pragmatic philosopher from Wisconsin who was afraid of Kant. Baumgarten, who played chamber music in a quartet with Erich von Holst, asked von Holst whether he knew a psychologist with a good foundation in biology who was interested in the "a priori," in one's innate nature. My name was mentioned and I obtained the position. It was there that I bloodied my nose, so to speak, in a head-on encounter with the transcendental philosophy of Immanuel Kant. It was also there that I wrote my first theoretical work on evolutionary epistomology for Karl Popper.

Now it so happens that new ideas grow, unnoticed, in the background, like mushroom spores underground. Then suddenly a mushroom springs up here, another one there, and all seem to be independent of one another. The mushrooms, the fruits as it were, symbolize people who all have become aware of an idea at the same time.

I have always said that I only preceded Karl Popper because I bloodied my nose on Immanuel Kant. However, this is absolutely incorrect: one hundred years earlier, Ludwig Boltzmann had formulated clearly the principles of the theory of evolutionary epistomology, saying, "What will become of the Kantian, apriori manner of thinking and viewing, since both evolved by confronting the real world."

At many times in my life, I have had good fortune, not good fortune through adversity but literally good fortune because of the previous existence of good fortune. For example, this situation happened with my first animal, the fire salamander. When I brought the salamander home, my father sternly ordered that it must be set free again after a week so that a five-year-old couldn't coddle it to death. My father believed that he could survive a week with me. However, what my father didn't think of was what we would do if the salamander reproduced. That was exactly what happened. The salamander was returned to the forest as ordered, but I kept the larvae, which of course deeply impressed me. I wonder whether or not a fire salamander could have had the same effect—in a positive sense—in one week as did the larvae, which needed weeks and months until their metamorphosis was complete. That is a long time for a child to observe and experience. Who knows what would have happened if the fire salamander had not had any young. Perhaps everything would have developed in a completely different direction.

If I had not had personal contact with wild animals I might have become an engineer.

# THE FAMILY HOUSE
## IN ALTENBERG AND
## FRAU GRETL LORENZ

*S*ince *you were made a professor emeritus, you have been living, with brief exceptions, in your parents' house in Altenberg, near Greifenstein.*

An incredible number of memories are connected with this house and garden: memories of how I began my work and of countless happy hours with my family, friends, and acquaintances. This house was built about the time that I was born. Before my parents began to build, we lived "just over the road," that is to say, in a country house on the other side, where the large aquarium now stands.

At that time, my father had just made the important discovery of how to help children with dislocated hip joints by using plaster casts rather than performing surgery. This, in turn, was linked to yet another stroke of luck: One of my father's patients was a very well-to-do lady from America, the daughter of a corned-beef multimillionaire. The millionaire, who was very concerned about his daughter, was apparently extremely pleased with my father's treatment, and he expressed his gratitude, among other ways, in the form of generous honorarium.

This seemed to go to my father's head somewhat, and my parents decided to build the house. However, for this awesome project, we needed, I must add, an accommodating architect because my father wanted the structure to be a mixture of Jugendstil and baroque styles. The fact that his wish became true was largely due to the fact that my mother on the whole was unable to interfere because she was preoccupied with being pregnant with me. However, my father's commission was nevertheless too ambitious for the architect, who literally went mad during the job—he became progressively paralyzed. The difficulties that he encountered during the construction were especially evident in the uppermost rooms. One of these was actually built with thirteen corners; I'm not exaggerating, thirteen corners. I myself lived in this room for a long time and believe that I emerged from the experience unscathed. My mother always used to say later on that the architect's illness increased with every floor and the deterioration was sup-posedly visible in the construction. My father was very pleased with the house, but my mother frequently said ponderingly, "Totally wrong, totally wrong!"

My acquaintance with my wife was directly due to our garden. We were neighbors and knew one another from pre-school age. My wife, whose maiden name was Gebhardt, was the daughter of a gardener who lived next door to us. The gardener's foreman, Herr Lose, always brought Gretl with him on his bicycle whenever he had to work in our garden. Seen in this way, Herr Lose was a very important person in my life. I can still see Gretl sitting on the Gouvernail. My wife seems to have inherited her gift for gardening. If you look at our garden, it is largely the fruit of her effort. She has the marvelous gift of keeping the garden in a half-wild state; her great secret consists of transplanting from the Viennese forest plants that multiply by themselves.

Of course, I played with Gretl a great deal as a child. We pretended to be Indians and animals. When we grew older, a number of other men were interested in her, but we were largely inseparable. When my father saw this attachment, he sent me to study in America for awhile, thinking that we would forget one another by the time I returned. That, however, did not occur, and since Gretl also began to study medicine—it was still quite unusual in those days for a girl to study medicine—he soon consented to our "friendship." Gretl became a very good and very gifted gynecologist, and was the family's breadwinner at the beginning, since at that time my studies and observations brought in no money. However, somehow, in some way, we were always able to get on and make ends meet. Even to this day, Gretl's hospitality is praised to the sky by all those who know her, including all my former students and friends who have visited us in great numbers and always have been served tea and a hearty meal. In this regard, I recall that Gretl recently said, "It's wonderful to realize that all of the people who used to visit us long ago are now doctors and professors."

It truly has been a good and full life. Gretl has never let herself be overcome by circumstances. One time, when she was already very pregnant with one of our children, she had to go to the hospital to perform a rather difficult operation on a woman whose pregnancy was also far advanced. Afterward when I asked her how it went, she replied, "Not badly, except that our stomachs rubbed one another somewhat." My wife especially shares my love for dogs. We once had a guest who was so impressed by this that he said, "Frau Professor, I would like to be a dog in your house!"

# · LIVING ·
# WITH ANIMALS

*A*  *s a specialist in comparative animal behavior, you have kept animals and observed animals during your entire life. You must have experienced a lot with your pets.*

First of all, I must say that I didn't begin keeping animals as pets just when I needed them for my research; on the contrary, I have been very close to animals since my childhood and throughout my entire life. It was certainly of immeasurable value to me that I lived by the meadows of the Danube and had the Viennese forest practically out the back door. In addition, we also had a large garden with lots of different creatures that crept and flew, all of which made a strong impression on a preschool child.

My first animal was a fire salamander from the Viennese forest, but we have already talked about that. After that, I had ducklings, which I raised myself. I remember very well that I was a well-fed child, because my mother thought that tuberculosis was the result of undernourishment. She was especially pleased when I took a second helping as a means of preventing tuberculosis. Children, of course, quickly take the path of least resistance, and when I wanted my parents to consent to my having a new pet, I prefaced my request by asking for a sandwich, knowing that I would more easily attain my goal. I must admit that my parents were very tolerant in this respect. As I grew older, I had a most diverse assortment of animals.

At that time, I did for fun what I do now as research. My instinctive curiousity as a boy developed gradually into more formal research. Scholarship arises from play. It's a fact. Today, I must confess, I suffer from time to time from the fact that I plan too many things and must devote myself to solving problems rather than to the animals themselves. From the very beginning, I did a lot of things right, either by chance or by instinct. I always have maintained that in order to get to know a higher form of life, you must live with the animal. The arrogance of today's researchers who believe that they can answer every question by examining an animal experimentally was always foreign to my nature. The truly interesting questions only arise when one has become directly acquainted with animals. One must live in close contact with them, which, of course, requires a significant amount of self-sacrifice, since higher animals and little children are strikingly similar in one respect: Both develop a tremendous desire to do precisely that which they are not permitted to do. This, of course, leads quickly to difficulties.

I remember that I kept a mongoose for quite a while. A mongoose is a lemur, a semiape. The problem with the mongoose was that apes cannot, in principle, be house-trained. The kitchen was one of the places where he was forbidden to go. However, one fine day, he managed to get into our kitchen. Since the mongoose is a highly intelligent animal, he was, of course, immediately interested in everything new. He found a huge kitchen knife used for cutting meat so interesting that he took hold of it. When the cook discovered the mongoose with the knife in his hands, she ran screaming through the house, afraid that the ape would do her harm. Her fear was groundless, of course, since the animal could not know that he held a weapon in his hands. However, it is very difficult to convince one's shocked household help of such a fact.

I recall especially fondly a colony of freely flying jackdaws, which I kept in birdhouses in our loft. They were the subject of my first scholarly work. I was extremely fortunate to devote myself to jackdaws first, for even today I can scarcely imagine a beginner observing a better research subject for animal sociology. I also loved my colony of night herons in the garden. When I had guests, I always could impress them immensely by saying, "And now I'm going to make a night heron appear!" Then I called out, "Go-ogg, go-ogg," and a night heron flew out of the spruces. I threw him a fish, which he caught on the fly, and then he disappeared with the fish into the tangled spruce branches. It was really a beautiful sight. The night herons were indeed among the finest animals that I ever studied. Unfortunately, they are also linked with a sad story, since all of the notes that I took about these extremely interesting birds were lost during World War II, and today I don't remember enough to write something scholarly on them that would be worth reading. That is over, however; those stories I shall take with me to my grave.

I have so many notes on geese that I could fill an entire room. I am resolved that my next book will be about them. Once there was a duck and goose pond in the garden, which I had dug myself. That was a very long time ago—it must have been in 1935 or 1936. I had many different kinds of ducks then. My father loved geese, and I had one that was exceedingly tame. This goose would follow me into the house, which was quite a feat because geese are visibly ill at ease when they don't see the sky over their heads. We also had a gander who was not so tame but was so fond of this goose that he overcame his fear and followed her into the house. However, being in the house caused him so much anxiety that his bowels were stimulated and he defacated profusely, which, of course, was not very good for the carpets. You can still see the spots. Thereafter, if I remember correctly, my father was less fond of the geese.

Later, when I had my institute in Buldern, all of my assistants, like me, were such passionate lovers of animals that our diverse menagerie almost got out of hand. This can easily become a problem and one should not underestimate it. There was a real danger that our research institute would be transformed into a zoo or an ark in short order. We recognized this very quickly and so we swore to one another by all that was holy that each would keep only those animals that were necessary for his research. One easily can see that if everyone also kept animals for pleasure, our researchers would soon become animal keepers. The oath that we took was so solemn that we almost signed it in blood, and, believe it or not, we actually kept it.

However, the love of animals cannot be valued highly enough, especially for amateurs. For me, the word *amateur* is by no means negative, for amateurs can become true specialists who do a tremendous amount of good.

A few years ago, a man requested an appointment with me. When he arrived, I asked what I could do for him and he explained that he had a plan to breed barn owls. This was, of course, an extremely laudable plan since these beautiful nocturnal birds of prey are becoming increasingly rare. Raising barn owls in captivity, however, is really one of the most difficult tasks of ornithology. Up until recently, it was equally difficult to breed grouse; that is, black and wood grouse under the care of humans in a way that was good for their species. Anyway, we discussed the most appropriate size of the volary and the best method of breeding. I bade farewell to the man, wishing him success and all the best without, I must confess, placing too much hope in his project. A few years later when I had almost forgotten the matter, the same man asked to speak with me again. When the day of the meeting arrived, I asked, not without certain malicious thoughts, "Well, how many barn owls have you bred?" "Forty," the man replied. I was, of course, deeply impressed and, moreover, ashamed, because one should not underestimate an avid animal lover. Anyone who keeps animals learns that one should not give up quickly, not even in an apparently hopeless situation.

Many years ago, I ordered a toucan, a pepper eater, from a pet shop. Toucans have huge beaks in comparison to their bodies, and I was particularly excited since I had never had such a bird. When I collected my ward at the train station—he was sent to me as freight—I made an exceedingly sad discovery: The bird sat completely exhausted on the bottom of the cage, resting his head on his monstrous beak. His eyes were half-closed. In short, there were signs that he was at death's door. The toucan must have been left outdoors during the night, and the cold had badly harmed this denizen of the tropics. Needless to say, he wouldn't eat. I had no other choice but to stuff him; that is, to force-feed him.

That night, I left him in a warm room. The following morning, I went in, certain I would find a bird corpse. Something completely different had happened, however: I saw a bird that both aroused my sympathy and appeared ludicrous, a bird that was busily studying the world outside his cage. The toucan was utterly denuded. The shock of the cold air had caused him to molt suddenly and lose all of his feathers; the picture that he presented was scurrilous indeed, especially given his enormous beak. However, the worst was over. A few months later, when all his feathers had grown back, I had a magnificent toucan who gave me a great deal of pleasure for a long time.

I have seen unusual things, or, rather, had rare experiences with animals very close to home. I remember once taking a walk in the woods near Vienna and encountering a ring snake that was eating something. What was it devouring: a fire salamander! It had swallowed the salamander headfirst so that only the hind legs and tail still protruded from the ring snake's mouth. That is extremely curious, since a fire salamander is poisonous. If you squeeze a fire salamander in your hand, it excretes a substance from the glands that begin behind its head and continue along both sides of its spine. This whitish excretion greatly irritates our mucous membranes. If you touch your eyes, nose, or mouth after "playing" with a fire salamander, you will not forget the experience. What is true for a person is also true for a dog: If you take a young, inexperienced dog on a walk in the forest and he ferrets out a salamander in a moist ditch and begins to paw at it, he will soon run to his master, howling piteously, with mucus running from his flews.

The dog won't make the same mistake a second time. Of course, this secretion is part of the salamander's defense: The salamander, like all amphibians, tires easily and cannot run away quickly enough. This, by the way, is due to the fact that its circulatory system mixes blood that is rich in oxygen with blood that is deficient in oxygen. The same is true of frogs and toads, which tire after a few leaps. However, although the fire salamander is inedible—a fact that is signaled by its bright colors of warning—this ring snake devoured him. I swear that I'm not making it up. I saw it with my own eyes. Of course, these are exceptions that make an indelible impression on one.

I have wonderful memories of the time when the meadows along the Danube near my home in Altenberg were not yet destroyed by the dam. The summers in this almost primeval forest were marvelous. Shortly after the war, when I was released from being a prisoner of war in the Soviet Union, I owned a dog named Susi, a clever mongrel. Susi had trained herself so well that she knew that when I took a landing net and a container we were going to the Danube to fetch food for the fish in my aquarium. In those days, there were meadowlands such as one hardly finds today. Every type of animal lived there: kingfishers, orioles, herons, and many others. To judge by this unspoiled landscape, one would not have been surprised to find crocodiles in the quiet tributaries. However, on hot summer days, I was the only crocodile: I spent hours in knee-deep water, lazier than a crocodile, watching my dog chase mollusks and muskrats.

Apropos of crocodiles, my friend Bernd Hellmann once had an alligator. Mind you, alligators don't bite—they bite as rarely as ring snakes. But I committed the most common of all scientific mistakes, namely that of generalization: I assumed that crocodiles also don't bite. One day I was in Bernd Hellmann's room when he wasn't at home. In order to pass the time, I went to look at his terrarium for a while. There, next to a marvelous Mississippi alligator, lay a green Nile crocodile of a similar size. I wanted to touch him and *snap,* it was hanging on to my finger and twisting lengthwise to tear out a piece of flesh. Just as I succeeded in extricating my hand, Bernd came in and began to laugh hysterically. He had made the same mistake with the same painful results and had just returned from the hospital with his hand in a sling.

Touching animals, having a physical contact with them, is, to a certain degree, a part of man's experience. No one would keep a dog or a cat for very long if he couldn't touch it. With some animals, however, this can have serious consequences, as in the case of the crocodile. However, physical contact becomes truly dangerous only when the animals attain a certain size.

There are other saurians, such as monitors, that are carnivores and that attain a considerable length. The Komodo dragon, for example, grows to be two meters long. It is, of course, horrid and despicable that the natives on the island of Komodo, where these reptiles live, tie goats to posts so that the dragons can tear them to pieces. This gruesome show is only staged for tourists. However, these dragons can also be dangerous to humans.

Once when I was abroad, I was the guest of a zoo that had a huge terrarium, almost as large as a house, with Komodo dragons. The director of the zoo, who was showing me about, was visibly surprised when I asked to go near the Komodo dragons—a male and a female. I went into the terrarium and on a spontaneous impulse lay down on my stomach on the back of the female. She liked the warmth of my body, since all reptiles are cold-blooded—their body temperature changes with that of their surroundings. Suddenly I couldn't breathe, because the male had climbed atop me. I had become a Komodo dragon sandwich! I can remember looking out of the corner of my eye over my shoulder and seeing the long, fleshy, forked tongue of the male flicking past my head to my hand. He probably thought that I was a guinea pig or a rabbit; that is, a meal. I was a bit uncomfortable. Of course, he couldn't have devoured me, but there are more pleasant things than being bitten in the hand or somewhere else by a sizable Komodo dragon. However, it ended well and I succeeded in leaving the terrarium without a scratch. The zoo director was a little pale, though.

I kept wild animals at home from time to time—wild not in the sense of aggressive but in the sense of not domesticated. Do you know the freshwater aquarium that at the moment is full of algae in the sun room? Next to it is a little marble basin, which is now dry, with the rather tasteless grotto and statue of Venus. There used to be water in it and I kept dabchicks. What delightful animals! I let them fly about the room, and even in here where we're sitting. What was unusual about them was that they learned to land on the water of the marble basin. That was a real achievement because it is incredibly difficult for birds to comprehend that the surface of the water is suddenly higher than the ground around it.

I have cared for a great variety of animals during my long life. A newspaper reporter once asked, "Tell me, how does your wife like it with a houseful of animals?" I answered in jest, "She doesn't see them; she works in the hospital during the day." Seriously, however, it wouldn't have gone at all well if my wife hadn't understood. She gave me a great deal of support and developed a love for the animals—especially for the dogs.

I have a truly marvelous story about the time my wife and I were in Hawaii. One magnificent tropical evening, we went for a walk to the edge of a forest with one of the people from the biological station. We heard the most wonderful sounds that you can imagine from animals that are active at night. I said to the woman who was accompanying us, "Tell me, what bird is that we hear singing?" The woman answered with certainty: "That's not a bird; that's the sound of a frog!" Not half a minute later, the "frog" flew over our heads. The moral of the story is that even an expert can make a mistake.

These people showed my wife, among other things, a bird spider. Bird spiders are gentle and do one no harm. Gretl was courageous enough to allow them to put one of the spiders on her hand. Suddenly, however, she had a spontaneous reaction to shake the spider off. There's nothing one can do to stop it—it's a natural reaction to surprise. However, the bird spider flew right into the face of the person who was showing it to us—an awkward situation indeed!

Nowadays, our house is pretty quiet. There are the dogs and the thrushes, which are already singing about the arrival of spring. Down below in the large aquarium, I have ocean fish, primarily coral fish. At present, I have more than one hundred fish of some thirty-five varieties. Otherwise, I can only mention my latest achievement: completely ordinary canaries. My friend Jürgen Nicolai gave me a wooden bird cage for my eightieth birthday; in it, I keep canaries. Anyone can raise them without difficulty, but I am as happy as a child about having them; for me, every animal is a slightly less gifted but very likable colleague.

# PART TWO

# Observations on Living Systems

*"... chaos is
indeed the
devil."*

# THE CREATIVITY
# OF PHYLOGENESIS

*P*eople have known at least since Darwin's time that nature
is not static. Evolutionary processes and mutations are both
ubiquitous and quite frequent. They "create" species, "spe-
cialize" them, or make them "disappear." Like a believer filled with
doubt, one is forced to ask why?

If man hadn't continuously asked questions from the very
beginning, there wouldn't have been any progress. When scientists begin to ask questions about phylogenesis, they discover
extremely peculiar, circuitous paths of development. It can
indeed occur that nature's "plans" are used for a purpose other
than that for which they were "foreseen." It's as though one
had a castle that was built solely as a castle and that is suddenly
used as a monastery or a school.

This is precisely what we find in phylogenesis. The trigger
for such a change of course is often to be found in creativity—I
avoid using the word *invention*. We strive to make discoveries,
to invent things, when the situation, a new situation, requires
change. Take the example of a fish's air bladder. The air bladder's original function was as a breathing organ, made neces-

sary by freshwater pools that were deficient in oxygen. However, the air bladder fulfilled two functions: First of all, it helped the primitive amphibians to breathe the air of the atmosphere and thereby to take over the land. Secondly, it permitted the fish that remained in the water to build skeletons of bones. Before the "discovery" of the skeleton, there were only cartilage fish such as sharks, since without the buouyancy of the air bladder, a skeleton of bones was too heavy and the fish would have sunk to the bottom. The "discovery" of the skeleton spread throughout the world's oceans because the air bladder rendered the fish light and unencumbered in the true sense of the word, while the framework of bones made the fish more stable. Amphibians that went on land are, of course, the predecessors of all land mammals, including man. Seen in this way, the air bladder is one of the most important developments.

The most laborious zigzag path of phylogenesis was that which led land mammals back into the sea again. I'm thinking of whales and seals, but this was also true of reptiles, sea turtles, and crocodiles. One has to remember that these mammals adapted to the water so completely that a nonbiologist would, in the case of the whale, think that creature was a fish. The path from a fish to a primeval amphibian, on to a reptile, then a mammal, and then back to a creature dependent upon water for its existence is an incredible odyssey. As for possible errors of evolution, I share the opinion with many colleagues that the path that evolution takes is almost certainly dictated by chance. It is precisely this chance that is rewarded in a particular genetic change in the snapshot of a specific environmental situation with the advantage of selection.

The record of countless genetic changes and selection processes is stored in the genome, but it cannot be recalled in the order in which it was recorded. That is the decisive point: Because of the inability to "remember" genetic changes, it becomes impossible for a creature to retrace a path of development. This is the state of knowledge about phylogenetic processes. The more specialized the adaptation of a creature to the ecological niche that it fills in an environment, the more precarious and uncertain is the continued existence of this species; the higher the degree of specialization, the less the likelihood that the creature can regress if this should be necessitated by a change in the environment.

In the extreme case, the variety or species may disappear. If the species should regress, then as a rule it is by another path than that which a combination of factors dictated. This is seen in the example of the sea robin, a saltwater fish. This species is the descendant of predecessors that, because they lived on the bottom of the sea, did not develop an air bladder: They simply didn't need to be able to float freely anymore, and the air bladder atrophied. However, if the sea robin were to develop into a species that could swim freely, it would not redevelop the former air bladder but would reshape it as breast fins. It would use these as a sail or wings in order to propel itself through the water almost as well as with an air bladder.

This is one possible path of evolution. However, the process of development can also end badly for a species, since highly specialized creatures can barely find the chance to circumvent such threats. Take the example of the blue throat, a beautiful bird that lives in swampy ground and eats only insects. If the swamp is drained and turned into farmland, the blue throat is unable to change its way of life and begins eating seeds and nesting among the potato plants. Another example is the swallow: This species of bird is in principle very successful and much more widely spread across the northern temperate zones than the blue throat. Now swallows do not leave for winter quarters because of a decline in their food supply; their migration is set in motion by other factors. For this reason, more swallows die than any other species of bird when the late summer is rainy and there are not many flying insects. Swallows are so highly specialized for this specific type of food that they are incapable of flying to the next anthill to pick ants out or to eat insect larvae from a tree's bark.

One can compare the extreme adaptation of a species with the risk that a manufacturer takes when he produces an unusual article without knowing how long it will be in demand. Imagine that the machines used to produce the article can scarcely be used to produce anything else. The analogy between the manufacturer and the specialized animal lies in the high, short-run profit. This short-lived advantage is enough for evolution, which does not make prognoses.

Human civilization and the conditions of life are changing so rapidly all around the world that phylogenetic evolution, the development of a species, is becoming practically irrelevant. It is as though the evolution of phyla stood still. Of course, there are animals that will survive because their degree of innate specialization is so high. In reality, these are not specialists like the swallows but omnivores like rats, foxes, and badgers. I heard lately that there are foxes and badgers—not to mention rats—that raid the garbage cans at night in the pedestrian shopping zone in Munich.

No one knows what will happen to those species that survive despite this pressure of selection that humans exert. We know only that the process of degeneration follows very soon. This is demonstrated by every modern breed of dog that has been highly inbred. As far as the future of evolution is concerned, one can do no better than to quote Manfred Eigner, who said that it is "a game in which nothing is certain except the rules of the game itself."

# THE RECOGNITION
# OF HARMONY AND
# DISHARMONY

*M*any people lack an appreciation for the beauty of nature.
One notices this especially in those who grew up in cities,
those who can no longer appreciate the harmony of the
countryside, the croaking of frogs and the like.

The ability to consider something beautiful and harmonious is
a triumph of our organs of perception over the analysis made
by our brain. This achievement is called perception of shape
(Gestalt). Such processes are characterized by the fact that they
do not originate in our sense of reason but result from amor-
phous reason or fuzzy logic. We know this, among other
things, from the work of Karl Bühlers. This means that these
processes are completely inaccessible to clear self-perception.
In other words, the perception of shape is based on an unconscious collection of sensual impressions. These impressions are
stored in our brains and suddenly—as though there were a

sudden flash of light—are connected to one another and thereby lead to a new realization. The closest comparison of this process is with the operation of a computer, except that the perception of shape results in what we call intuition. This is, of course, completely unconscious to the person involved, who feels as though he had received an inspiration from without. However, this is not a miracle in the literal sense but, rather, the simple accumulation or collection of data. However, even the perception of shape requires, like every other activity, training or learning.

There is a marvelous and true story about Franz Joseph, the Emperor of Austria, who was entertaining the King of Siam. The entertainment included an opera. When the opera was over, the King of Siam was, as propriety dictated, asked which part of the piece he liked best. To everyone's amazement, he answered, "The very quiet part before the curtain went up." It turned out that he didn't even mean the overture, but the tuning of the instruments!

Of course, it would be wrong to laugh at the man, because African and Near Eastern music is as inaccessible to us as an opera was to the King of Siam. Have you ever heard Turkish music? It is a cacophony in which an Occidental can hear no rhyme or reason. Otto Koenig, who traveled widely in Africa and the Near East, is familiar with this music. Once he took the trouble to play tapes of "good" and "bad" Arabic music for me; that is, more or less classical Arabic music—an Arabic Beethoven as it were—and trivial Arabic music. I can assure you that I couldn't hear any difference. Otto Koenig asked, "Don't you hear that one is awful?" To this, I replied, "No, the classical composition sounds just as awful to me." This was, of course, because I knew both types poorly or not at all, and so I couldn't relate to either one.

So it is with the optical harmonies that we perceive: the beauty of nature, the beauty of the forest, the beauty of the landscape. It requires training—the perception of shape—in order to distinguish between them subconsciously. Only when one is ecologically well versed, when one knows the difference between landscapes that are natural and harmonious and ones that are brutally exploited, does one learn, through one's subconscious, to distinguish between harmony and disharmony. When you travel through East Germany to Berlin, you see wheat fields stretching across the horizon. These fields have huge bare spots where the seed didn't grow. Such a landscape is positively ugly. On the other hand, one observes the landscape in Tullnerfeld (a region near Vienna), where the wheat grows well, where one can see that man lives in a harmonious equilibrium with nature even though the land has been cultivated.

One perceives the Rhine valley or the Wachau in Austria—where there are so many grapevines that one couldn't plant another one, where there remains no free soil, where the entire landscape reflects the influence of the vineyards—as beautiful, and our reason confirms that which we perceive with our senses. One perceives this landscape as beautiful because man and nature in this region are in equilibrium, because the interaction between man and nature can continue for centuries. One can continue to cultivate grapes in the Wachau for centuries and nothing will change. In contrast, the agro-industries of North America, Eastern Europe, and the USSR—and unfortunately also in West Germany—appear to have plundered the land and appear so ugly. Our perception of shape says, This cannot continue.

The lack of crop rotation becomes a curse for future generations; this is true not only with farmland but also with forests and everything else that is subject to single-crop farming. This ability to recognize an equilibrium in nature, which is necessary for the proper functioning of our perception of shapes and the harmony of our senses, is probably the prerequisite for the preservation of nature. By such recognition, man thereby realizes by himself that he is not diametrically opposed to nature but is a partner, a beneficiary and a member of the framework of life. In discussing music,

I already have suggested how this can be achieved.

My friend Eberhard Stüber, the successor of Paul Ewald Tratz, runs the Nature House in Salzburg and is head of the splendid Salzburg Young People's Organization to Preserve Nature. He has experience in interesting children in nature and considers nature hikes just as important as musical education. I don't know whether a musical education alone is sufficient to enable a person to perceive harmonies in general, but it certainly helps. The better one knows landscapes and ecological systems by heart, the more sensitive one is. This sensitivity enables one to recognize automatically the smallest disturbances or disharmonies. I could almost say that one is like an experienced, venerable conductor who does not fail to note the slightest discord in his orchestra. This perception of shape can, of course, be applied to science; in fact, it is indispensable for science.

In American psychologists who study only rats and conduct experiment after experiment to train them, we have an example of how science can go terribly awry without such perception. It is a frightful mistake to experiment with only one type of animal. I can say from experience how important it is to know different types of animals in order to discover commonalities. Had I not observed the most diverse types of birds and fish, I would never have discovered the analogies between, for example, pomacentroids and gray geese or jackdaws, or between cichlids and geese. There are indeed similarities, for example in the way they defend their young. The duck provides a superb example of this. During my entire life I have kept and observed all kinds of ducks. While observing them, it suddenly occurred to me that in certain situations the drake unfurls his wings and, "trrrt," brushes his beak across his pinions in a sort of cleaning movement.

I suddenly had the feeling that I knew that movement, that I had seen other aquatic ducks make it. Suddenly, out of the clear blue sky, I knew which aquatic ducks make the same motion: all of them! It had not caught my attention before I saw the garganey; even though I had observed it with many other aquatic ducks, I had not been aware of it. However, my subconscious had noticed the motion and frequently had recorded it in my memory. I can't explain why it first occurred to me while watching the garganey, but probably this observation had made the cup overflow as it were, causing recognition to arise from experiences, forming a synopsis out of elements that had been isolated up until then.

The perception of shape is also important in medicine. Unfortunately, this fact is increasingly underestimated by today's doctors because they believe that they can rely more or less one hundred percent on the most modern diagnostic equipment. Of course, it is a blessing that we have such modern equipment, but one should not underestimate the so-called clinical look that the old general practitioner still has. Such a doctor immediately could observe: "The color of Mr. Smith's face has changed. I have known him for twenty years." Today, a doctor unfortunately cannot have the same personal relationship to a patient that a doctor had fifty years ago. Nevertheless, I consider it essential that a doctor record information over a longer period about patients whom he knows well. This gives rise to the "clinical look," which signals the smallest changes in a patient's health.

The odd thing about the perception of shape is that one is notified only of the result and not of the path by which one arrived at it. Look at the example of the garganey. We know that the mind's ability to absorb and preserve impressions is much more complex than we previously thought. As I have said, the term *perception of shape* can, simplified, be considered the continuous collection of data on diverse topics. And, as I already mentioned, the perception of shape tells us whether or not a landscape is healthy and beautiful, whether music is melodious and pleasing.

However, even here there are differences. When a beautiful animal film shows—especially in slow motion—a jellyfish swimming, apparently weightless, its transparent body expanding and contracting in a marvelous rhythm as it propels itself through the water, then hardly anyone would fail to find the harmony of the movement graceful and beautiful. However, when you see pictures of the same jellyfish stinging a swimmer or a snorkeler who did not see it and swam into its tentacles, when you see the swimmer's skin turn burning red, you feel an intense disruption of harmony. You feel more sympathy with the human than with the zoophyte, which perhaps will be destroyed.

It is very similar when you examine a fungus mycelium. Seen alone under the microscope, it is a wonder of nature how the tiny branches form a harmonious unity. However, when the fungus infests poinsettias on the windowsill so that the beautiful red bracts wither, one cannot help but empathize with the relatively higher harmony of the plant and react against the relatively lower harmony of the fungus, which is now considered a parasite.

One can, therefore, say that one of the most important achievements of the perception of shape is the distinction between sick and healthy or, analogous to it, beauty and harmony from discord and ugliness.

In addition to this, there are other attainments of the perception of shape that are based on the same principle as the computer mentioned earlier, which can only give the optimum results when it is supplied with a great deal of data. Take this page of paper. The fact that you see it as white in the reddish light of a light bulb, in direct sunlight, or in the bluish light of hazy days is a result of this extremely complicated subconscious process. If I take my glasses and begin to turn them in front of my eyes, I see the resulting foreshortening but not as a distortion or shortening of the object that I am looking at. However, if the lenses expanded and contracted by themselves, I would throw them away in fright. It is not our sense of logic that executes these processes but, rather, the perception of shape.

*It follows from what you have said that the perception of shape plays an extremely important role in questions of environmental protection or in the global destruction of the environment. Should a person who understands the harmonies of the world in which we live want to strive to prevent their destruction?*

Yes; this should not be underestimated. Some time ago, questionnaires were mailed to Nobel Prize laureates who were biologists, ecologists, and zoologists and to academics who were active in these fields. Among the questions that the specialists were asked to answer was when they had first begun to take an interest in nature, animals, and plants and when they had first come into contact with living organisms. In essence, this question was designed to determine whether or not the scientists had had contact at a preschool age. Do you know how many had? All of them! All of them had had contact with living beings in some form or another from their earliest childhood. This means that their perception of shape was intensively fed with data about nature. One can feed one's subconscious with all sorts of things. Demagogues, lobbyists, and advertising people know this best of all. Those who are blind to values, and this group includes almost all important politicians and industrialists, usually grow up in big cities where their perception of shape included very little of the beauties of nature. A person who has seen only skyscrapers thinks that only skyscrapers are beautiful and does not consider a little village whose architecture blends well with the surrounding landscape to be beautiful. Modern architecture is by no means blameless in all of this. If you look at a cancer under the microscope, a cross section with cells of healthy tissue, it looks exactly like an aerial view of a city in which the old sections are surrounded by new, irregularly built regions or else by those that are monotonously geometric—both are possible, after all. The parallels between the formation of malignant tumors and cities in a state of cultural decay are very wide-ranging.

You find the highest incidence of crime in the ugliest parts of town. The Neuerlaa district of Vienna is both the police commissioner's biggest headache and the ugliest thing that was ever built in Austria. That such a thing could have been built is explained among other things, by the fact that architects have grown blind to natural harmonies, to perceiving harmonies with their senses. That doesn't have to happen. One could do something.

One only has to familiarize children and young people with harmony so that they aren't blind to values; in fact, so they won't be able to live discordantly. One has to be trained to be able to distinguish harmony from discord, however. The very thought that more and more young people are growing up in big cities is extremely frightening. I confess that I feel guilty when I think of these young people, because I was able to grow up in harmonious surroundings. How will they ever become responsible and especially prudent adults who as politicians and businessmen will direct the destiny of the earth's biological totality when they have never learned what the beauties of nature and their harmonies mean? Keeping Leghorn hens in cages is, without a doubt, cruel, yet humans are to be degraded to living in cells of concrete blocks? This can't go on.

One cannot forget or overlook the fact that man by his very temperament was not created to be an interchangeable, anonymous unit as is the case with worker bees or worker ants. In the latter case, when one creature dies, the next carries on in just the same way. A good example of this is seen in small gardens where people who are still partly receptive to harmonies employ the most diverse forms to express their unique individuality. No two small gardens are identical; each one is the expression of a different set of ideas.

Therefore nature in harmony and a harmonious—in the sense of beautiful—environment are equally important for man if his soul is not to be damaged. I tried to make this clear in my book *The Waning of Humaneness*. The essence of this book is the enormous loss of the sense of harmony in today's society. In the final analysis, it is always blindness that is responsible for the shattering of harmony, which then brings misfortune. This breeds chaos, and chaos is indeed the devil.

# PART THREE

# The Misuse of Creation

*"One needs to
take many
pictures of an
animal, a
landscape, or a
biotope so that
one can tell a
story—a story
that ends almost
tragically but
that finally has
a happy ending.
One should do
this so that one
understands
what was
almost lost."*

# ON THE
# HUMANIZATION
# OF ANIMALS

*We attribute human traits such as pride, stupidity, arrogance, and cunning to animals. However, their behavior is determined by the demands that prevail in the biocenosis and cannot be compared with the conscious actions of humans.*

Yes, that's the old evil division between useful and harmful. This division has taken root so well that it has actually become one of the greatest barriers in spreading understanding of the community of life. It has become characteristic that, as a rule, the good and useful creatures are those that can be eaten. Rabbits, stags, and does are very good. However, one cannot, for example, eat a fox. I haven't tried it; I have had to eat dogs and cats, but I haven't tried to eat fox. Fox meat supposedly stinks so badly that it's simply inedible, and that is certainly one reason why a fox is considered evil. This division into good and evil animals is a kind of humanization: Man and animal are juxtaposed as though they were on the same level. However, when a fox goes hunting and kills a hare, it is not considered the same as when the forester goes into the forest and shoots one, but, rather, as though the butcher killed the baker and roasted him! In reality, of course, this is absolutely wrong, since the fox needs to feed on a hare from time to time, whereas the forester hunts a hare for sport and enjoyment. He could just as well eat beef or pork, which we can raise.

Unfortunately, however, one doesn't look at it this way and so a false image of an evil enemy arises, which is expressed in the term *beast of prey*. Many biologists, therefore, pedantically call these animals hunters or predators. Most people don't see that in a natural environment the prey is, to a certain extent, dependent on the predator, his natural enemy, in order to maintain the ecological balance. People think in clichés: Inane films and deceptive novels by sensationalist producers and authors much too frequently depict wild animals in a manner that is strangely enough preferable to the public than is the truth. Take the lynx, for example: It is frequently considered a wild beast—you hear this said often over a glass of beer in a pub— that eats oxen and humans and similar nonsense. A lynx can indeed be very dangerous when attacked, but so can I!

If you come at me with a knife, I'll shoot back without hesitation. The maximum size of a lynx's prey is predetermined and small enough that it would never attack anything larger than an adult doe. However, when an animal is driven into a corner and wounded so that it can no longer run, then— take the example of the rat—it reacts with a furious counter-attack. Of course, the lynx acts in the same way. I absolutely don't believe that a lynx that was not wounded has ever attacked a human in an open hunting ground. I'll eat my hat if that ever has happened. Recent studies have concluded that there is no documented case of wolves spontaneously attacking humans because of hunger. I don't believe the story of a wolf pack running behind a sleigh, which is a classical motif in Baltic tales. That may have happened in the Middle Ages, before there were firearms and when people had only bows and arrows, but as far as I know, there is no documented case. One must remember one thing: If there were lynxes and wolves in the forests again, they would have a healthy effect on the deer population. It's an illusion to think that hunters completely replace these beasts of prey, since they shoot almost exclusively fully grown stags.

There are hunters who perform their art in a truly conscientious and noble manner. Of course, one cannot talk of "the hunter," because that's the same as talking about "the man," "the woman," "the Englishman," and so on. There are extremely good and sensible hunters. Nevertheless, by his very sense of sight, smell, and hearing, a hunter is unable to distinguish an inferior from a superior animal, as a beast of prey *can*. The sparrow hawk, for example, immediately sees which quail in a group of quails is the weakest and attacks it. Because of his inferior senses of perception, the human hunter is unable to do this as quickly and is unable to determine his notch and sights with the same innate ability.

My dogs once brought down a roebuck—an old animal—whose teeth were worn down to the gums. Even a dog chooses an animal that is weaker; the primordial hunter, the wolf, is particularly good at this. Very exact studies have been made about the relations between the wolf and elk. On the Ile Royale, on a large lake in Canada, studies were made of the native wolf population, which functions to a certain extent as "elk breeders" during the span of a good thirty years. During this lengthy period, the island's wolves never brought down a healthy, strong elk. The scientists who studied them flew in a helicopter to the site whenever the wolves had brought down an animal. They found that the wolves killed only calves that had been dropped late and wouldn't have survived the winter or old elks that were starving.

Everyone knows that nature is merciless. Do you know why an elk dies? An old elk starves to death because its molars have been ground down to the pulpa, after which the gums break open and become horribly infected; the elk's gums hurt so badly that he doesn't eat enough. The old elks that the wolves of the Ile Royale had killed were almost exclusively those with such fistulas in their gums. Seen in this way, the prey is to a certain degree dependent on his natural predator, which selects the weak and the sick to the benefit of the rest of the population that is strong and healthy.

This interaction between hunter and prey is not limited to carnivores but is also found among plant eaters. There are various hoofed animals, for example antelopes, that prefer a certain type of grass. Such types of grass, in turn, require that they be kept short by being eaten and trampled on. If these factors are absent because of a lack of animals to eat and trample the grasses, they are soon supplanted by other types that are naturally ranker. The same is true of English lawns: Only by continuously mowing them can they remain thick and free of weeds. As soon as one ceases regularly to mow the grass, plants are supplanted by others, with the result that one soon has a meadow of dandelions and daisies, which I happen to prefer but which I doubt would please, for example, the gardeners of the Schönbrunn Palace in Vienna. One can say, therefore, that an English lawn interacts optimally with a lawn mower. A natural example of the same thing are the meadows near the Alps where beautiful orchids grow because there are cows and sheep that keep the grass short. If there were no animals, everything would be overgrown and the vegetation would change very quickly.

It is an interesting fact that one carelessly judges the character of an animal by his appearance. Everyone at the zoo wants to pet the bears but no one wants to pet the hunting leopards because they seem so athletic compared to the funny bears. This has led to frightful accidents with bears, which have bitten off children's hands like straws when the parents weren't being careful. Bears don't live, as people like to think, on sugar provided by wild-animal tamers; they're carnivores and have the teeth for the job. We have the same problem in natural parks: It would be better if the larger wild animals remained afraid of people, because when you feed them, when they seem to be tame and come near the hotels where tourists can photograph them—as one can in Yellowstone Park—that's when they become dangerous. Wolves aren't dangerous, but large bears are, and during the last few years grizzly bears have frequently attacked and killed people. For example, a sleeping man was dragged out of his tent by a bear without the second man in the tent even noticing. The bear had reached under the tent and seized the man's head, probably had bitten into his brain, dragged him into the open, and ate him. Grzimek would say ate and not devoured; so a bear ate a man.

One has to expect such accidents when one tames wild animals so that tourists in shorts can photograph them without a telescopic lens. When one doesn't shoot the large beasts of prey, then the latter begin to understand that people are completely harmless. One should, therefore, maintain man's reputation as the most dangerous beast of prey by shooting a bear now and again, although bears are too beautiful to be used as rugs in front of the fireplace. The best solution would be not to tame them at all so that there would be no accidents.

*Another distinction is between intelligent and stupid animals.*

One of my teachers, Hochstetter, used to become furious when one spoke of primitive creatures. He always answered, "There are no primitive creatures, only higher and lower forms of life." It is completely incorrect to say that a goose is stupid or a fox sly. It's not only incorrect but it's also not interchangeable. No animal is sly or stupid in the sense that humans are. Every creature is adapted to its environment and endowed with characteristics that ensure its survival in the niche that evolution has provided for it. Anemones, zoophytes, are not less intelligent or more stupid than a raven when viewed within the context of the world in which they live. Of course, it seems primitive when an anemone sits on a coral reef, immobile—as far as the reef is concerned—dependent on the currents for its nourishment. The raven, in contrast, seems very intelligent when it examines its pieces of food and is capable of significant learning processes. Zoophytes and vertebrates differ in what they do to survive in their surroundings.

What happens when a higher form of life "artificially" lands in the realm of a "lower" form is seen in the case of the dingo.

Dingoes were originally domesticated dogs that became wild in Australia. Judging from their innate ability, they were more intelligent than similar predators, such as the Tasmanian wolf and the Tasmanian devil. Both the Tasmanian wolf and the Tasmanian devil were, given the anatomy of their teeth, superior to the dingo and could have bitten him to death without difficulty. However, things turned out differently: Both marsupials required, given the way nature made them, a relatively dense population of animals on which to prey for their very survival. The dingoes, however, had a more advanced brain and were much more strategic hunters. They could survive with many fewer animals on which to prey, animals they could track down much better. So it happened that the dingoes weren't wiped out by the animals that were better fighters; rather, the reverse happened: The dingoes thinned out the prey to such a degree that the Tasmanian wolf and Tasmanian devil couldn't find the remaining prey quickly enough and starved, as it were, with their plates empty!

Nevertheless, it would be categorically incorrect to call the Tasmanian wolf and Tasmanian devil stupid. They were able to live very well in their surroundings for thousands of years with their relatively primitive brains. Only when the dingo came, which wasn't an organic part of nature in Australia at all, did these native predators lose the competition with a more "modern" animal. Put another way: If the dingo had come to Australia little by little and in small numbers, the Tasmanian wolf and Tasmanian devil might have had time to meet the challenge of this more intelligent competitor. As it was, everything happened almost like lightning and there was no time to adapt. The Tasmanian wolf and devil only exist today in Tasmania, where no wild dog populations were introduced.

We have the same problem with many types of wild animals when humans change the world in which they live. Take the example of the great bustard, one of the largest birds in the world that can fly. The great bustard lives exclusively in the steppe, where there are no obstacles such as large trees or fences. When one plants a windbreak in the open to counteract erosion so that the soil will not be blown away, then the great bustard will disappear, because it is irritated by forests or rows of trees. Simple fences such as one has in a pasture are death traps for this bird, which flies against them and literally breaks all his bones simply because such structures in the landscape have not been recorded in the great bustard's genetic code. The process of mutation, which would take account of changes in the surroundings, takes a very long time. People alter their world much too rapidly for certain species to adapt apace. It is by no means incorrect to maintain that, globally speaking, man plays the role of the dingo.

*Last but not least, we attribute character traits to animals.*

The knowledge of certain mechanisms that trigger our instinctual desires to care for something was used very early by the doll industry: Large, large, relatively deep-set eyes, rounded cheeks, and short, thick extremeties are the ingredients for producing saleable dolls, because their appearance appeals to people by awakening their innate instincts.

Traits such as these have been intentionally bred into certain breeds of dogs like the Pekinese and the pug, with which childless women express their need for love and affection. It is, of course, a sad side effect that these poor animals that are already deformed are also usually overfed and made neurotic. As for such sweet and cute creatures in a broader sense: It is an amazing fact that certain animals that we want to consider cuddly have names with a diminutive ending that say that they're cuddly: squirrel (Eichhörn*chen*), rabbit (Kanin*chen*), robin (Rotkehl*chen*). The diminutive ending says nothing about the animal's size but identifies it as cute.

The degree to which we allow ourselves to be deceived is seen in the cuddly squirrel, which is also considered to be hardworking because of the way it gathers. Aside from that, no one would ever imagine that such a funny little animal could be cruel—again from a human point of view. It is hardly known that squirrels are not only vegetarians but also carnivores, at least as an occasional addition to their diet. It happens that these rodents raid birds' nests when they find them: Not only do they eat the eggs but also the young and, when they can catch them, the adult birds brooding the eggs. They eat them skin, feathers, and all. By raiding birds' nests in this way, squirrels have at times done great damage to the population of songbirds. No one would believe that such a cute animal is capable of such a bloody act, because it looks so nice.

Other animals don't appear nice but, rather, arrogant—think of the camel or the llama. The reason is that their nostrils are higher than their eyes and the corners of their mouths drop. We consider people who bear themselves in this way to be arrogant also. In the camel and the llama, this expression is by no means an indication of their temperament; it has an anatomical origin. The counterpart is the golden eagle, which is found on countless coats of arms. The Habsburgs esteemed the golden eagle because it looked so proud, so intelligent, and so reflective. This is born out by the bird's anatomy. The crests of bone above his eyes give him a fierce look, and people compare this visage with the wrinkled brow of a thinker. In addition, the corners of the eagle's mouth are drawn to the back, which reminds us of fierce resolution.

All the external traits just mentioned, which induce us to draw conclusions about the character or humor of an animal, really refer to humans and are not transferable. In conclusion, I repeat: The camel and the llama always look at you the same way. When you want the llama to eat from your hand and the llama wants to spit in your eye, it won't look one jot unfriendlier; you can only recognize what he's planning by the position of his ears—which is certainly very different from a person.

# OBSERVATIONS
## ON NATURE FILMS
## AND PHOTOGRAPHS
## OF NATURE

*W*hat do you think of the value of nature films and photographs and books about nature in a world in which many people aren't able to see wild animals and unspoiled nature?

I must enlarge on that topic. One of the problems with people today is that most of them deal only with lifeless, artificial objects in their daily work, with objects that are not particularly beautiful and that are by no means appropriate to inspire awe and respect. That's why most people have forgotten how to live with living creatures, with living systems, and that, in turn, is the reason why man, whenever he comes into contact with nature, threatens to kill the natural system in which and from which he lives.

How one avoids this, how one can educate mankind not to destroy the environment—the direct consequence of which is self-destruction—how one can teach people to sufficiently respect very complicated systems of life and biological control systems—which they can not destroy if they want to remain alive—that is a task of educating the masses. It is a job that one can tackle in a number of different ways.

The media plays a very large, a dominant role. Picture books about ecological systems and nature films are an extremely effective means. These books and movies are used foremost to present nature to people. One must take into account that only harmonious, unspoiled nature is really and truly beautiful; the term *beauty* in the philosophical sense, of course, has many facets. Despite these many facets, today's older generation of industrialists and politicians, who shape the destiny of the world, remains ignorant of the beauty of nature. For this reason, the older I get, the more important it seems to me to preach about the dangers of ignorance and blindness toward the biological totality of our world. That which I preach is so simple that every seventh grader can understand it; namely that every exponential economic growth, every growth that requires the use of energy will lead to catastrophe in our finite world. It is inevitable.

To a certain degree, the older I get, the more radical I become in protecting the environment. However, during the last few years, I have grown less pessimistic than I was, because I see now that my sermon, along with those of other people who also understand, are meeting with an ever greater echo among young people. More and more young people feel obliged to emphasize what I just said, to teach the public at large about nature and respect for nature. These words are directed at a film that my present young interlocutor and a like-minded friend made. It is a film about nature and not, like so many films, about the cameramen or directors.

In a film about the Himalayas, it is, of course, essential to see what the mountain climber does, how hard it is for him, and what he must do to succeed. However, in a film about nature, about plants and animals, it is completely unnecessary to show how the film was made.

It gets on my nerves when, for example, in a film about Africa, I primarily see how bad the roads are, see the camera crew driving through huge puddles in jeeps, repairing the suspension or grilling a fish over the glowing camp fire. I recently saw a film like this, and it's a waste of energy to broadcast it.

Animal films such as your *Sitatunga*, however, are exactly the opposite of that which I just criticized. They are examples of what a nature film should be like. Whoever undertakes to make popular scientific documentary films must know a lot, must be both a biologist and a zoologist. It doesn't mean very much in a film about Uganda, for example, just to show the big game; it is equally important to show insignificant things such as plants or anything that is worth photographing. Of course, it is a lot of work to order everything that one has photographed and set it to music, but that is exactly what makes a good film on animals or nature. My wish would be that there would be many more films such as *Sitatunga*. There are many unknown landscapes, countless rare species that are becoming extinct. One would be occupied for years filming these things, showing them to people, or at least preserving them on film for future generations who perhaps will no longer be able to see them in their natural state. That is the job of nature and animal films. Unfortunately, because of television, much too much utter nonsense about animals is broadcast. I shudder when I think of one of the "Daktari" programs in which an ocelot was shown as a young leopard. Such things cause more harm than good, of course.

When a movie shows how the desert bursts into blossom after a rainstorm, accelerated with the aid of time-lapse photography and accompanied by classical music, such a film can indeed impart a sense of harmony even though it doesn't correspond to reality. The blossoms of the flowers open and close in a rhythm according to the brightness of the light, determined by day and night. Moreover, you don't hear Beethoven or Mozart in the desert; what you hear is a vulture or a falcon screeching here and there. However, when the desert is depicted differently than it in fact is, with blossoms opening and closing quickly accompanied by classical music, this can evoke genuine feelings and a sense of harmony.

The spate of animal movies that contain a plot have, on the whole, helped animals, because people become less willing to kill them; they think twice before destroying an animal when they have identified with an animal movie that has a happy ending. This naturally also happens with films that show scorpions "dancing"—that is, tottering back and forth—to waltzes, which, of course, they never do in reality. The important thing is that the film does not present anything categorically false, such as depicting tawny owls as young eagle owls. In such a case, the film's message becomes untrustworthy, like a politician who doesn't do what he has promised after the elections. No one trusts him the second time he runs for office. Thank God there are still people who can distinguish tawny owls from eagle owls. A film about animals cannot permit itself such deception because if it does, it becomes a bald lie that discredits other films in which the camera crew really braved the wind and rain to provide unusual scenes to the audience sitting comfortably at home.

It is by no means without danger to film a sequence in which, for example, a bear chases a cameraman in order to attack him. Grzimek's son fell out of a helicopter and died while making aerial photographs in Africa for the excellent film *The Serengeti May Not Die*. That is, of course, a great sacrifice. However, this film was so successful and touched audiences to such a degree that countless people stood up and said "Don't plow up the Serengeti." This clearly shows what a good medium an animal film is for awakening a deeper understanding of and a person's attachment to the wilderness and wild animals.

In addition, a good film about animals reveals much and renders much comprehensible that would otherwise remain hidden to people. Who can afford or is physically fit enough to dive thirty or forty meters down in a tropical sea to study a coral reef? A nature film allows us to see such things, just as my large saltwater aquarium does. I sit comfortably, see everything, and don't get wet—although I've never been afraid of getting wet. I have actually been diving and snorkeling, but my doctor has forbidden me to do that now. Sitting in front of an aquarium, or a television when there's a film about the sea— that's an old man's version of scuba diving.

It is, of course, incredibly important for science that we can record on film that which just happened and can reproduce this film as often as we please. One can say without exaggeration that a film about animals is to the behavioralist what a sample on a slide is for the anatomist. That is the essential element in modern science. When an animal—a goose, a wild boar—does something interesting that perhaps I have never seen before— believe it or not I discover new things almost every day sitting in front of my big aquarium, things that surprise me and for which I have no satisfactory explanation—and when by chance the camera records that, then it is an inestimably valuable aid because I can later analyze what has happened literally frame by frame and second by second.

If there's no way to film the event, I am compelled to wait for the animal to repeat its behavior before my eyes until I conclusively understand the meaning. Sometimes one has to wait a long time for such a repetition, perhaps even longer than the life span of the creature being observed. Much that animals do occurs incredibly quickly, and although the human eye can, of course, be trained to see the "right" things, there are simply limits to the ability of our senses to absorb information. Just as I cannot perceive viruses with my naked eye, so it is practically impossible to note all of the similarities in the simulated situations involving a chimpanzee stacking crates on top of one another or unscrewing screws in order to find the banana he desires.

Such situations are staged several times, filmed, and then compared in detail. In this way, one can see exactly what was pure chance and what the result of thought processes. This is why we have scientific films about animals collected in large archives. The Encyclopaedia Cinematographica in Göttingen is the leading institute of this type and the best example.

However, one must add that animal films for scientists can occasionally be dangerous for the specialists who watch them. It sounds incredible but it's true, because one accepts the random sample for the general rule. One has to be very careful in this respect; otherwise, one can be led astray very easily. The most common of all scientific mistakes is that of generalization. In the realm of comparative behavioralism as in the realm of comparative anatomy, it is a deadly sin. I remember, for example, that I always used to say that a ring snake *Natrix natrix* bites as soon as it has hatched. However, the young "ring snakes" that bit me were *Elaphe longissima*, young Aesculapius snakes! They resemble ring snakes to such a degree that I was fooled for a long time. Of course, there are slight morphological differences that, because I was generalizing—a young Aesculapius snake still looks like a ring snake when you look a second time—I had simply overlooked. The same thing occurs with animal films for specialists. What one has seen time and again becomes so imprinted in one's mind that one is drawn to see it as the solution to the problem even though it may not be. One needs to have a little distance, which one must cultivate.

Scenes in scientific animal films that are not staged and thus that show a certain exception to the rule are beautiful and of great scientific value. Once I saw a film by Jane Goodall, the specialist on primates, who only did field studies; that is, she lived with the apes, observed and filmed them. In the film, she showed that chimpanzees are not, contrary to popular opinion, exclusively vegetarians. I recall not without horror a scene that was both macabre and unique: One saw a dead member of the chimpanzee clan, or rather what was left of him—namely, the bare bones of the spine and on top the uninjured head, which looked as though the chimpanzee were sleeping peacefully. Another chimpanzee held this "scepter" with a head. While he looked at the face of his "sleeping" brother, the chimpanzee plucked the last bits of flesh from the spine and ate them with relish. It was wonderfully documented and macabre at the same time.

On the other hand, one must realize that a camera significantly limits, or even disturbs, the observation with the naked eye. Moreover, scriptwriting and filming are two completely different activities—which must be kept completely separate—in making animal movies. There is a big difference between that which one would like to film for a movie about geese and that which one finally gets in front of the camera lens. Animals, wild animals, are not actors who repeat a scene as often as the director wishes until the latter is satisfied.

It becomes very difficult when the animal notices that it is being filmed. Sometimes it begins to behave completely abnormally. My friend Peter Scott one showed us a wonderful film about a mandarin drake. While the film was running, I said precipitously, "Now the duck will do this and that." Annoyed, Sir Peter answered, "No. Now the drake is in focus and well lighted so that he will most certainly not do anything of the sort. Don't you know that?" Indeed, the drake didn't make the well-known mating movement that one would have expected.

Only in advertisements do animals behave differently; there, in front of the camera, we see cats eating "whiskies" and "friskies" that taste wonderful. Even if the cats aren't eating the cat food that is advertised but, rather, something else that tastes better—I'm convinced of this—still the animals are given nothing to eat for one or two days so that they run right before the camera and to their food, thereby helping the cameraman save film. Cats used in advertisements certainly must be kept on a starvation diet. In addition, one can do a lot with modern photographic techniques, with trick photography. Great progress had been achieved. I recall very well when Heinz Sielmann began to make films after the war. Everything was prepared with the greatest effort. The heavy cameras were brought into position and then, exactly at the most important moment, when the animals were doing the most important things, one heard "bzzz whirrrr hummm" and the camera broke down again and the entire reel of film was ruined. Filming is much simpler and easier today because there are fewer mechanical failures.

Personally, I always wanted to make a film on environmental protection—about the renewal of an aquatic biotope: a reservoir in a coal pit in the Ruhr region, showing how one plants its banks until reeds grow and mallards return again. In short, I wanted to do something simple. Then I wanted to return at regular intervals and film from the same spot so that in the final film, time would be telescoped. However, I would have had to begin when I was three, since a project like that takes eighty years. It even takes two hundred years if you want oaks to grow. Such a project would be appropriate for a father and son, since one lifetime is not sufficient. Such films in which time is telescoped would be very valuable, but so far as I know, they don't exist. One could show people very vividly how a dead pond in a gravel pit can, over decades, come to life again; that a biotope is a pulsating organism whose development is so slow that one cannot comprehend it clearly without telescoping time.

The same holds true for documentary films about large numbers of insects, such as ant colonies or swarms of grasshoppers—or even about people at the market square. If you film such scenes at a normal speed, you don't find anything unusual at all when you look at the film. Only when you telescope time and make everything happen much faster do certain patterns of behavior that are predictable begin to emerge.

The same holds true of the opposite: Slow motion is an equally valuable aid in scientific animal films. One can make truly remarkable discoveries with slow motion, as did John Burchard, for example. With the help of the Institute for Scientific Films, he showed the fuction of the chameleon's tongue. The chameleon's tongue is propelled forward by a ring of muscle, which shoots the hard, swollen part forward like a cherry pit. The insect at which the chameleon is aiming sticks to the end of the chameleon's tongue when it is struck. After the "hit," the tongue slackens completely, falls, and is retracted into the mouth, of course with the insect stuck to it. The action is so quick that one simply doesn't see it with the naked eye. With a slow-motion camera, however, we can study it clearly.

*Animal photography, however, is completely different when there are no moving pictures but only stills. The photographer must have a fine sense for choosing the right moment to shoot.*

This is very true. The first photographers of animals were, in a sense, stone-age men living in caves. They developed a photographic eye, so to speak, for the animals they hunted. This is beautifully seen in the numerous eidetic paintings of animals in caves. The animals are always depicted leaping, running, or at the peak of some movement. These animal paintings show that the artists, who were hunters, were more interested in animals than in men. In these paintings, prehistoric cows, giraffes, and bears are beautiful and are drawn with great understanding, whereas people remain only stick figures. Animal drawing, which is, of course, the predecessor of photography, is still of considerable importance for science. When I was much younger, I drew animals quite often. Sometimes they were only sketches, studies of the movements of ducks and of foxes when they pounce on a mouse. Sometimes I make line drawings for my books.

Now for photography as such: Photography is ideal for freezing action at the climax. Naturally, I realized very early on the importance of photographing animals as a document or evidence of a certain behavior. For this reason, I photographed a lot at the beginning, but then stopped because I always had assistants who were better photographers than I. I remember that I had a camera with two lenses, the kind you look through downward from the top. At that time, all sorts of animals were running about freely in my garden here in Altenberg. Among them was a colony of night herons that flew about freely.

I set my sights on one heron in order to photograph him. As I looked down through the camera and stepped farther and farther back in order to get a good picture, another one flew up and defecated on me—plop, right on my collar. That can happen when one is concentrating completely on the object that one is photographing and forgets one's surroundings.

Today, there are very few truly good photographers of animals, photographers who just go on safari in Africa to capture everything that walks and flies. Good wildlife photographers tend to become specialists: Each one concentrates on one thing—insects, birds, and so on. The result is photographs that say a lot about animal behavior. One has to add a word of praise: Photographers of animals really do require an animal's patience, since the animal is expected to do something special and be close and in focus, look nice and sit still in front of the camera. Of course, it doesn't always do that—doesn't swell its crop when it is in the right position.

Photographing animals requires, therefore, incredible knowledge. One has to know an animal's pattern of movement in advance in order to be able to predict roughly what each will do when. With a film, the pictures are continuous, and so it's somewhat easier to catch action scenes or mating scenes, but with photography, there is only one picture after another, and these must be planned precisely in order to be successful.

*Nature books depict almost exclusively an unspoiled world. One rarely sees a highway dividing the landscape or a dump disfiguring a summer meadow.*

I've realized that this problem occurs frequently in connection with Horst Stern's films and photographic documentaries. How much ugliness can a film or a newspaper permit without repulsing the average viewer or reader? It can easily happen that the viewer will say: "Must I really see this?" That's why a beautiful picture of an animal seems more effective to me, since it shows what we would like: to preserve beauty and harmony. But I think that it's a balance between minimum and maximum: How much suffering must I show to arouse sympathy, and how little suffering may I show, in order not to repulse people. People look aside all too easily. If people were not so skilled at looking the other way, one could never live in a small Italian town. There, the hens are hung upside down by the feet while still alive, and the horses, asses, and mules are brutally driven with stones and kicks.

However, beautiful pictures of animals and nature do a great deal to propagate and develop a sense of ecology. I recently heard, for example, that according to statistics, *National Geographic* is primarily read in the concrete jungles of New York City and Chicago, where on the fiftieth floor of a skyscraper urban people look at the beautiful photographs of mountains, forests, and lakes—in short, every thing that they don't have and can't get. Magazines such as this provide a substitute, and as such are not bad. They can never substitute for reality— there is a tremendous emotional difference between looking at beautiful pictures of a coral reef and diving down to see one oneself—but it is at least better than having absolutely no feeling for the beauties of nature.

Given our increasing urbanization and alienation from nature, we need beautiful photographs of landscapes and natural settings. Such sublimation is not, as I just said, a substitute for desires, but it helps, since, to quote Freud, "Only the unfulfilled person fantasizes." On the other hand, I am a bit divided, because, to be honest, postcard pictures of blue skies are not enough. An unspoiled world contrived by advertising executives and demagogues should not be propagated unconditionally. One needs to take many pictures of an animal, a landscape, or a biotope so that one can tell a story—a story that ends almost tragically but that finally has a happy ending. One should do this so that one understands what was almost lost.

Nevertheless, those who photograph animals are guilty of many things. They are, I may say, literally obsessed until they have taken the photograph they want and can go home in good spirits. Whether or not the frog dies shortly thereafter from an overexposure to flash attachments is secondary to them. I am convinced that countless animals have paid for a good photograph with their lives. That is indeed very interesting: Even as a child, I wondered as I looked at pictures what happened to the animals after they were photographed?

In the new Brehm, in the old new Brehm, there are many photographs taken by Heinroth of birds at various ages.* I didn't believe that these birds were raised so that a new picture could be taken every week or two. I believed that the birds were photographed and then destroyed. Even when I was twelve or thirteen, I couldn't believe that it was the same bird growing up. Yet Heinroth took care of the birds he photographed. One hopes that there are many photographers as conscientious as Heinroth, since it's horrible to think of mistreating and killing an animal just for a picture.

Ultimately, it's a crucial question. On the one hand, one is pleased when people become a bit interested in nature and animals. On the other hand, it is a horrible fact that a dear young sparrow must pay with its life for the stress of being photographed. It is perhaps irrelevant that one considers that one's photograph converts numerous people and motivates them to preserve nature and animals. Of course, the sacrifice of an animal can be legitimized, if at all, only if a photograph is used in a book that will be read by many people. However, if the photographer is actually a friend of nature and animals as he should be, then he will always be concerned from the very outset to preserve and protect.

*Trans. note: Alfred Brehm, Brehm's Tierleben. Allgemeine Kunde des Tierreichs; many editions were published between 1890 and 1925 but never translated into English.

# ON ADAPTERS

*S*tatistics tell us that every day several kinds of animals throughout the world became extinct, although we don't notice it because they are frequently unspectacular forms of life. On the other hand, there are also countless varieties that are able to adapt relatively quickly to cultivated, civilized land.

Both are processes whose importance one may, by no means, underestimate. For one thing, the extinction of a species is an irreparable act. When the last male and female of a species are dead, then that species will never reappear by itself: Only a new act of creation can recreate them. Whoever is aware of this should be deeply shaken, since simple reason should show one that Homo sapiens is also only one creature among many that needs water, air, light, and food—one should also not forget a cultural basis—in order to live.

Consequently, preserving animals from extinction should be one of our most important obligations, something of vital interest to us, since the resistance of every biological system increases with the number of species that inhabit it. That is true for a pool as well as for a complex coral reef or rain forest. That is the goal of the process of cognizance, which hopefully will not take too long to reach; namely that man is not above the laws of biology on earth with its different ecological systems. People live not only in deserts but on the North Pole and in jungles. The same laws of nature apply everywhere. That is why, as I mentioned, the extinction of a species of plant or animal is by no means so harmless as some industrialists and politicians think. On the contrary, it is extremely tragic.

There are certain things, however, that one can preserve and repair. Zoos are by no means unimportant in this respect. Of course, it is a very bad situation when a zoo does nothing but collect animals, much as an elementary schoolchild avidly gathers stamps from around the world. In order to be worth anything, there must be a certain system behind the collection. To put colorful birds together in a cage without any principle other than the fact that they are beautifully colored is senseless. Today, in particular, zoos should devote themselves to research and propagation of the species that they keep, since otherwise, the zoologists cannot bear the moral responsibility of putting rare animals in cages.

In other words, the idea that one is putting the last or the next to the last Bengal tiger in a cage, even though one knows that there are still more in nature that could reproduce, seems to me moral suicide.

However, there is the reverse condition; namely that the habitat of a species is destroyed and one preserves the animals from extinction by putting some in a zoo—to create something like the proverbial Noah's Ark until the danger is over. Good examples show that this is possible: Look at the *Oryx* antelope, the European bison, or the Przewalski horse. If there had not been zoos that had bred these animals until they multiplied into herds that could survive, they would doubtlessly be in a museum now.

When one can breed rare animals in captivity, one should do it. Unfortunately, many cannot be bred and I have only to go to my aquarium in order to realize this fact anew.

Of course, one can question the sense when the natural

habitat of a species is irreparably ruined. Then the animals would have to remain in a zoo as though in a museum forever. However, there is the justified hope that things could improve.

Some species cannot be bred or rather have not yet been bred in captivity. We can only help these animals by protecting their habitats. One cannot breed the great bustard because it inhabits the steppe and one cannot recreate a steppe in a zoo. These large terrestial birds need treeless expanses from horizon to horizon; that is the habitat to which they have adapted. They run against every structure they see, such as the wall of a cage, and die. This is only one of many examples of how even rationally conducted breeding in captivity cannot help some species because it simply doesn't work. In many other cases in which the animals breed in captivity, we still don't know whether they will survive in the long run.

There are animals that have adapted to the "borders" between different habitats; among these are the unlikeliest plant eaters. For example, an animal that eats everything that farmers plant in the Tullner field may die out if the field gets too big. The daily wanderings of a normal hare would not bring it to the edge of a large, industrially cultivated beet field. It is born into a single-crop landscape. The question is whether the hare, which normally eats a wide variety of plants and sometimes even mushrooms, can survive on sugar beets; probably not. Viewed superficially, the hare is an adaptable animal that follows civilization. Nevertheless, the hare not only suffers from farming on a large, technical scale but is even in danger of being killed by it.

We know from experience that there are animals, for example certain birds, that are able to adapt readily—flourishing in city parks and on garbage dumps. We know that there are birds that benefit greatly from large, technically run ports. It is an interesting fact that a port causes bird colonies to die out in a circuitous manner by means of other birds that follow civilization: One of the most difficult problems of protecting the birds of the North Sea is the fact that the silver gulls flourish so well in the large ports that they do serious damage to the breeding grounds of the terns and other birds that breed along the coast. The fact is that silver gulls live on refuse such as the remains of fish generated by a large port. The gulls multiply dramatically and then attack the nests of eggs and the young of the other shorebirds.

One of the principal methods of protecting the birds of the North Sea coast is to shake the gulls' eggs so that the embryos die and the gulls spend a long time trying to hatch them. The fact is that these shorebirds count instinctively on floods and quickly build a new nest, with the result that there are even more silver gulls. The problem posed by the silver gulls shows very clearly that adapting is a very touchy matter.

Various ducks provide another good example. Take, for example, the mallard's tremendous ability to adapt, or on lakes, the tufted duck. I can observe this phenomenon right near my home. If you look at the dam at Altenwörth, you would think that the tufted duck was created specially for dams, because it does so well. Other ducks, such as the red-crested pochard, are not very common. The key thing is that we don't know why. No one can tell you why the mallard adapts so well to civilization while its closest relative, the pintailed duck, cannot. However if you breed both kinds on ponds, you will at least recognize this fact. No one knows the reason, but the mallard is easy to breed and the pintail very difficult. No one can tell you what the effects will be when the pintail dies out. I must emphasize once again that no one knows what consequences the extinction of a species will have on the interrelations of a biotope. This is a warning that can at any time have negative effects on man, even though such effects may not have been so apparent earlier.

Curiously enough, certain predators have also adapted very well to cultivated fields and civilization. I could write a utopian novel in which the fox, which is widely considered to be shy, moves into the suburbs, where it lives in the sewers and feeds on the garbage of the slums. The same is true of the badger, which has migrated to the suburbs, where it empties garbage cans at night. Or beech martens: In some areas, it has become difficult to park one's car on the street at night because beech martens come and not infrequently bite through the ignition wires. Those are phenomena of the last few decades. Where they will lead to no one, as I said, knows, which is not without danger. I recall, for example, that on excursions to Neusiedler Lake forty or fifty years ago, people were extremely pleased when they saw a coot. A coot is a rail, and rails are actually very shy. Today one finds coots even on artificial ponds in parks. So one sees how much can change during a lifetime.

The big question is whether or not such adaptations are really beneficial over the long run. There is no doubt that it's extremely good to hear that peregrine falcons nest in the big cities in Germany and raise young. Although they traditionally bred on rocky cliffs, they have adapted and build their nests on the rocks of cathedrals. That, however, is not the end of the story: Peregrine falcons are not omnivores that can be pleased as easily as ravens and gulls, which brings me back to the food chain, where adaptation can bring doom. Most predators—using the example of the peregrine falcon—have a certain hunting pattern. In other words, a *Falco peregrinus* won't look for grasshoppers and worms in a field as a buzzard will; it hunts game birds, usually as big as doves. It's favorite prey include quails and partridges. Quail are especially valuable for eliminating insects. Now if partridges and quails, which are already greatly endangered, live on fields where potatoes are grown with agro-industrial methods, they will primarily eat the archenemy of farm crops: the Colorado beetle and its larvae. Then comes the high-tech farmer in his "crop duster," raining thick clouds of insecticide on the fields. Aside from the fact that many insects that are considered farm pests have, to an alarming degree, become immune to the insecticides used against them, nevertheless since they are lower insects, they can, without a doubt, tolerate more insecticide than higher birds. The ability of the Colorado beetle to adapt to insecticides is downright frightening, and one reason for it is that the time span between generations is much shorter than that of its archenemy—the partridge—and so the partridge east poisoned beetles. The insecticides are not readily degradable in the bird's body; then along comes the peregrine falcon and catches the partridge, which has been weakened by the insecticide. This illustrates the process of selection whereby the slowest animals become a predator's first prey. The peregrine falcon or its brood become the last host of the insecticide, with tragic results. Studies have shown that poisoned peregrine falcons become sterile or their eggs' shells are too thin, which means that when the bird broods its eggs, they crack. A severe poisoning with insecticide causes the older birds and the young in their nests to die. In this way, the insecticide destroys the peregrine falcon's closely interlocked food chain. The Colorado beetle's successful adaptation leads to destruction. That is only one example of the negative effects of adapting. One must now reckon with the fact that man is often at the end of a long food chain, the effects of which are seen dramatically in heavy-metal poisoning caused by eating fish from the Baltic Sea.

One can also not ignore the incredible ability of rodents such as rats and mice to adapt. A mouse can eat almost everything. Despite the most clever methods, man has not succeeded in eliminating mice because they, probably the most typical of all animals that follow civilization, can adapt to practically all the changes in their habitat. The amount of food that mice and rats take from the starving people of the Third World is certainly enormous. Research in evolution teaches us that a species can most easily adapt when its degree of specialization is low. A chameleon is dependent on eating moving insects since its specialization is connected with motion. A mouse, on the other hand, is neither choosy about what it eats nor where it lives. Nevertheless, there is a great imbalance between those species that can adapt to changes in their sorroundings and those that cannot. One can name only a few animals that can survive when their natural habitats grow smaller; that is to say, ones that can move into town with us. Most species are certainly unable to adapt as rapidily as the changes in civilization require.

If things continue as they have up till now, then many species will not survive into the next century. In particular, birds, many of which have adapted to highly specialized circumstances, will be affected, although I think that seabirds will not die out entirely. They will continue to live in the Nordic regions, although they will probably disappear from the European coasts. However, the sea eagle, for example, as well as other birds of prey that are linked to the water, are in great danger. In my youth, there were tremendous numbers of black kites living on the Danube, and today one doesn't see a single one. Regarding the mammals that live on the sea, it is sad to say that the otter will soon disappear. This is largely the fault of fishermen, since fishermen are much worse conservationists than hunters. Hunters know what sportsmanlike conduct is, whereas fishermen are so consumed by professional jealousy that they even shoot kingfishers because they eat little fish. As far as ducks are concerned, the mallard mentioned earlier will probably continue to flourish, as will Nordic geese that live in freshwater. So will the mute, which is multiplying.

However, to look into the future and determine what will still exist and what will not is impossible. One cannot foresee a prevailing ecological social structure. If there are feudal lords and aristocrats, for example, they will strive to have the stag survive so that they can continue to have pleasure in hunting.

# · GENE · MANIPULATION, DOMESTICATION, AND GENE LOSS

*I*s it possible that there will be "monsters" one day when scientists begin in earnest to breed plants that are specially adapted to withstand their environment? Or will we see especially resistant animals needed for the recultivation of completely devastated regions?

I think that is unlikely because first of all, there is too little time. The only things that develop quickly are symptoms of degeneration, the breaking down and loss of genes. You can see this degeneration in every breed of dog that is modern and strongly inbred. However, I think that it is practically impossible that a new and, in particular, a large form of life be created in civilization.

On the other hand, there are no bounds to science and things can always be discovered, but quantitative science errs when it believes that research, which focuses increasingly on reductionism, can offer a genuine solution. Many natural scientists, in particular many molecular biologists, believe that the explanation of complex phenomena can be found in reduction, in detail. However, one cannot say that the processes of life are only chemical and physical; they are that, too, but one can only understand the system when one arrives at an understanding after reviewing all of the components. If you want, for example, to understand the law of gravity, you must not only know that there is a pivoted axle, a pivoted angle, and a bob but you must understand the interaction between all three. Only then can you deduct the law of the pendulum.

Thus, I don't believe that everything will continue as it is now, including the fields of domestication and gene manipulation. I wouldn't sit here and talk if I did not have hope. That's why I am not very frightened by gene manipulation. Gene manipulation will only have the power to do something when humanity has grown wiser, and about this trend I am actually an optimist. I consider the possibility that something will be created that will destroy humanity to be as unlikely as the possibility that a dog breeder will breed lap dogs so dangerous that humanity commits suicide in sheer terror of them. This danger is not very great at all.

The real danger that I envision is that of genetic loss, which is frequently underestimated. We have to watch out. Genetic loss is sometimes even desired in pets, at least in the first generation. However, in succeeding generations, the loss can be so great that the genetic system as such ceases to function, with the result that animal breeders try to crossbreed primitive breeds of pets or even wild animals in order to compensate for the genetic loss that renders strongly inbred forms unviable. The same is true of plants. Breeding plants for the highest yield frequently lowers their resistance to parasites, with the result that one has to cross the houseplant with a wild variety that is more resistant to parasites in order to make the former more resistant. Then, suddenly, the wild variety is no longer to be found because all of them have been destroyed.

Therein lies a great danger. I hope and believe that animal breeders are already afraid because there are too few varieties due to the fact that domesticated animals have suffered genetic losses. My friend Hüthmayer had the splendid idea of making a sort of preserve for domesticated animals on an alpine pasture on the Kasberg and financing it with money from tourism. There, varieties of cows and sheep that are nearing extinction and that one hardly can find on a farm today are kept alive through traditional methods of animal husbandry. However, even if animal breeders don't realize that one shouldn't eradicate all the breeds of domestic animals, then at least the veterinarians are very aware of it, even if the original breeds provide less meat and so on and are increasingly supplanted by modern breeds. The former should not be eliminated, however, because the high-yield breeds always need to be rejuvenated with genetically rich and undegenerate varieties of their own species.

The same is true for all wild animals.

As the areas left to nature grow smaller, then even wild animals inevitably inbreed, with the resulting danger that even wild species degenerate. It is odd and distressing that wild breeds are sometimes undermined by their own domesticated varieties, which drive them to extinction. One can observe the beginning of this development very clearly in the mallard. The mallard has learned to follow civilization; it lives in lakes and ponds in parks where people feed it and it lives well alongside the domesticated white duck that also inhabits these spots. One may find both the wild and the domesticated varieties living together on ponds and streams near farms. They get along so well that they breed with one another and little by little the pure wild breed disappears.

One sees the effects of degeneration due to breeding in captivity in those wild animals that have a short life span as opposed to those that live longer. There are, for example, certain highly social varieties of fish that possess a very strong brood-care instinct. One has only to breed these varieties in captivity for a few generations for them to lose this instinct almost entirely. You hardly can find a pair of fish that is capable of properly caring for its spawn. That should give us pause.

Domestication not only produces major changes in instincts but occasionally also in appearance. Anyone who has an aquarium and breeds guppies knows that. The first batch of guppies is usually beautifully colored. However, if the fish crossbreed among themselves several times, an extreme loss of color occurs. If you then compare one of these fish with one that has just been caught in the Amazon, there is literally no comparison.

That, as I said, is what happens to wild animals. Curiously enough, people always tend to consider the wild varieties beautiful and noble and the domesticated varieties significantly less noble. I like to illustrate this fact in my lectures by using examples. On the left, I show a wild boar, on the right, a farm sow; on the left, a wolf, on the right, a lap dog; on the left, a wild carp, on the right, a veil tail, and so on. There is hardly anyone who doesn't consider the wild variety more beautiful. The typical characteristics of domestication—excessive fat, paunchiness, loss of muscle tissue, changes in the skeleton, such as a shortened base of the skull—are considered ugly. There is, however, one exception: If you juxtapose a picture of a wild horse, of a Przewalski horse, with a full-blooded Arabian stallion, then you will need some time to realize which is the wild and which the domesticated form. In the case of the Arabian stallion, man didn't want to breed forms with fat or a mountain of meat because, in contrast to cows and pigs, the stallion wasn't meant for food but for fast riding.

People today also display the previously mentioned characteristics of domestication, such as an increase in fatty tissue. One talks of a "prosperous paunch," but today even that is considered unappealing. Even sculptors in antiquity knew this: If you look at Greek statues, you will see that exactly those parts of the body that are most likely to grow fat are presented as especially muscular. One wonders to what degree the signs of physical degeneration are linked with the decline of ethical values that is characteristic of people today. When an old man collapses from heart failure in the New York subway, there is almost no one who will help him in a humane manner. In many places, indifference has reached a level and assumed forms that are frightening in the extreme. I consider these symptoms of degeneration, which cause the humanity in man to diminish, thereby causing the decline of culture, one of the greatest dangers for all of humanity. This problem has occupied me for a long time and I discussed it in my book *The Waning of Humaneness*. If humanity was to commit suicide, it wouldn't have to smother itself with a lack of oxygen because we destroyed the jungles and algae, nor must we voluntarily expose ourselves to radioactivity; it is enough that modern man dismantle all of his noble human values. One must warn people of this menace just as much as one must warn them of all other elemental dangers to the environment that our civilization has conjured up.

# MAN AND FOREST

*The destruction of forests, which has been caused by various aspects of our civilization, has become one of the major problems of our era—perhaps even an eschatological problem. Whether with power saws or air pollution, wouldn't you say that we are felling our future along with that of the trees?*

One can indeed say that without any exaggeration. Forests are the green lungs of Europe and every civilized country, and the destruction of the forest is so frightening because one doesn't know where or even whether it will end. Even if we were to radically decrease or put an end to acid rain, there is still a danger that the forests would continue to die. However, there is still hope. Fortunately, trees reproduce rapidly with seeds and reforestation can bring back some of that which has been destroyed. However, it is possible that the death of the forests causes other living things to die—such as vegetation in general, which can have catastrophic results for man. The ingrained opinion that man and nature are diametrically opposed to one another is as prevalent as it is disastrous. Most people adhere to the erroneous belief that all of nature could be ruined and yet man would live on. That is one of the main problems; if such thinking didn't exist, people would have become concerned about the forests long ago.

The relationship between man and forest is one that has occupied me greatly. The relationship assumes a special form in Europe, especially in German verse. In German romantic verse, the forest is glorified.

Strangely enough, the opposite is true in America. Today, many Americans still have a certain feeling of enmity toward the forest. Only a few generations ago, Americans were directly exposed to the forest's dangers and had to clear them to survive. The average American was extremely happy when a tree was removed That is, of course, the most shortsighted nonsense that one can imagine. In America, the forest is still something of an enemy for many people. Just as it seems impossible to protect wolves, which are the archenemy of sheep farmers, so it seems impossible to protect the forest. In connection with this, one should not underestimate the role that emotions play in economic life. In America, people are trying to pass laws that will forbid the cutting down of old trees in big cities. I don't know to what extent these efforts will be successful. What I know with certainty from my own experience is the following: In the eastern part of America, there are no large trees, only second-growth forests; that is, very thick forests composed only of small trees. These trees grew wild where farming was uneconomical because grain was grown too cheaply on much larger farms in the west. For a long time, I thought about what was lacking in the landscape of the eastern part of America: Large trees are lacking! Sometimes one finds only the trunks of large trees in the midst of inferior evergreens as evidence that the area was once farmed. These second-growth forests are inhabited by fauna, which is particularly interesting because these animals have migrated back again from the west, where they were once driven by the agriculture of the east. When you drive through the eastern part of the United States, you see many skunks and racoons run over by cars. Although this may seem interesting, this new ecosphere of small predators and shabby, inferior evergreens is somehow unsatisfying to the aesthetic sense of a Central European. If I was to give free reign to my feelings, there would be only "mixed forests" in Central Europe, which could grow and reproduce without the intervention of man.

A mixed forest has, of course, great advantages from an ecological standpoint. Every intact ecological system—and mixed forests with little systematic forestry are still largely intact ecological systems—is stable in proportion to the number of species of plants and animals that inhabit it. One example: If you take a mixed forest, it will not be destroyed by a plague of caterpillars, of course—something that would kill most of the conifers. A pure conifer forest, however, literally can be devoured by such a blight.

I occasionally like to quote Professor Burian, a botanist in Vienna, who once said, "Man's original sin is monoculture, the cultivation of a single plant for economic reasons." This is true for the forest as well as for fields. That's why a mixed forest, which is characterized by the diversity of plants that comprise it, is of great value, aside from the fact that it also provides the animal world with an incredible number of niches in which to survive. In addition, such a mixture is also pleasing to the human eye.

*There are, however, types of forests here that did not arise because of a monoculture but that still exhibit a natural limitation of the types of plants. For example, the lowlands.*

Yes, one could say that the lowlands are a limited mixed forest. As you said, they comprise only a few plant species. However, they are distinguished by the fact that they are perfectly natural and are especially demanding in terms of certain conditions. In order to function faultlessly, for example, lowlands require an annual flood, but they also offer certain advantages, such as their ability to regenerate quickly. If you have a completely barren area such as a sandbank, which consists only of sand and gravel, it takes only two consecutive years of no intensive flooding for willow seedlings actually to take hold. If willow seedlings reach the age of three or four, they can survive every flood and a fertile lowland will then emerge from the barren gravel. This is the basis for our hope, that in spite of the hydroelectric dams, certain tracts of lowlands will get enough water to survive and regenerate themselves. This is something we can win.

The value of the lowlands lies primarily in its fauna. There is hardly another habitat in which so many interesting—and unfortunately endangered—species live as in the lowlands. I am speaking, of course, about myself, since the lowlands are really my true home. This biotope is not only threatened by the dams in the inhabited areas; because they must be flooded every year, the lowlands are also, for example, incompatible with farming. In other words, one cannot cultivate a field in the middle of the lowlands. Once they are dried up by the dams, then all subsequent economic considerations counterindicate irrigating them. Those who direct the economy will say that frogs, toads, and mollusks, as well as "surviving Neanderthal men"—by that, they'll mean us—are not of sufficient economic value to render their preservation desirable. Such a sentiment can be found in a published article by a gentleman whom, for the sake of discretion, I shall not name. To that kind of thinking, I can reply that these "Neanderthal men" include, strangely enough, at least four Nobel Prize winners and practically all the intelligent biologists whom I know. I would like to emphasize that I feel very comfortable in the society of "Neanderthal men."

I opposed the Hainburg dam because I had the impression that the public utilities didn't understand how important this habitat is. I received a letter from an important representative of these utilities who revealed through his thoughts that he didn't have the slightest inkling of what was at stake. I would have considerable regrets if our government was to issue a permit for Hainburg, and I know that at least a few of the most important members of the government would not do so wholeheartedly.

Unfortunately, I can see before my very eyes the shocking destruction caused by the Greifenstein dam, which swept away the lowlands right near my home. This happened in areas that are capable of regenerating themselves, but before they can, there will probably be factories, construction, and roads there. Nature preserves are urgently needed to protect various species of plants and animals so that devastated areas can someday be returned to their natural state. My friend Otto Koenig was quite correct when he pointed out that there exists something called "secondhand nature." Barren areas in Germany—especially gravel pits and the dam of the River Inn near Passau—have been transformed by conservation into new living biotopes. However, one can create these artificial biotopes only if one has a supply of natural biotopes on which to draw. The lowlands are one of the last of these in Central Europe.

If I thought that people would preserve those lowlands that still exist and that are unspoiled—for example, on the Danube above the Greifenstein dam—I wouldn't have opposed the Hainburg dam as I did. However, I am firmly convinced that all economic considerations that favor a dry lowland over a natural one will cause the disappearance of all of them whenever they are near a dam.

It is possible that some people want to eliminate all natural forests. That would be a catastrophe, a catastrophe of the most horrible dimensions. I wonder whether the monoculture of the artificial forest planted by foresters can survive in the long run.

At first, it seems that a forest consisting only of spruce or other intermediate trees is viable; Nor is it unattractive—the lower Alps are almost exclusively spruce forests—but the aesthetic value of a forest that is planted in ranks and files is diminished by this very fact. However, the monoculture forest is not lacking just in aesthetic value: There are ecological, biological laws that govern the entire world and from which businessmen with all their capital cannot ransom themselves. These forces are at play in a monoculture forest: The susceptibility of a habitat to "tip over," as those who have an aquarium say, is inversely proportional to the number of species that inhabit it. It can easily lose its equilibrium. A forest without any underbrush hardly can offer small animals, such as birds that eat insects, a place to live. When this underbrush is lacking, harmful insects are not eaten and therefore gain the upper hand. That is enough to start a vicious circle. One doesn't notice it right away, but such a situation harbors a great danger.

In addition, spruce and fir tend not to push their roots down very deeply, with the result that in a very bad storm—the kind that occurs every twenty or thirty years—monoculture forests are knocked down like matches because there are no other trees with deeper roots to hold up the spruce and fir by intertwining with their roots.

The thing that most harms monoculture forests is harvesting. This is done very quickly and is a blow to the animals, which are already too few in number. For the same reason, it is not good to reforest an area immediately after trees have been felled. Of course, the reforestation prevents erosion, but it's bad for the animals.

There is a law that requires the immediate reforestation of cleared forests. This is detrimental to animals, because clearings where all the trees have been cut are quickly overgrown by blackberry brambles and similar plants that provide food for deer. One of the reasons why deer—not to mention wild sows—cause damage is that there are too many trees in the forests and not enough plants that provide food for the game. Therefore, the animals are compelled to feed in farmers' fields at night, where they do considerable damage.

I am firmly convinced that the economic reasons for planting a monoculture have a purely commercial origin and that the very people who should know better have no idea of the true damage that they are causing.

A person's attitudes are formed very early; for example, by the anxiety generated in some children's books that have become very popular. Tolkien's *Lord of the Rings*, which almost every child has read, is such a book. There, the forest is considered suspicious, sinister, the abode of frightening spirits and is, on the whole, demonized. Such false, fictional views of the forest are very dangerous.

Although it may seem to contradict what I have just said, I must add that the image of the individual tree in our emotional world appears to be much more favorable. If one has grown up in a garden with old trees and has climbed old trees—my grandchildren climb trees in my garden that were planted not by their father or their grandfather or their great-grandfather but by their *great-great-grandfather*—and if I may consider my family's experience typical of that of other families, then I believe that people possess a great and apparently innate love of individual trees.

Such a garden gradually becomes a forest, since the trees grow older and larger—like my garden, which is over one hundred years old. If you want a meadow and flowers to grow, then you must sacrifice a tree from time to time so that the sun can reach the ground. It is characteristic of our family that when my wife and I go into the garden with our children and grandchildren to pass the death sentence on a tree, each tree there will have an advocate among the family. There will be one person who will swear by all that is holy that a particular tree may not be chopped down and who will marshal concrete arguments in favor of such an opinion. The large Caucasian walnut in front of my window renders my room almost uninhabitable in the summer because the leaves make it truly dark and gloomy. However, it would be murder to chop down this tree. By no means! That would be the worst type of vandalism. People who do not share these values are foreign to me—I simply can't understand them.

On the other hand, I know that there is a question of education involved. Young people who are imprisoned in a big city can't help the fact that they don't love trees, because they don't really know them. One needs good teachers and, better yet, good and understanding parents who take children out to show them the beauty of trees and forests. I think that people no longer know how to walk in the forest. This inability to interact with the natural environment has increased; yet walking through a forest in the right way is the best relaxation a person can have. The best way is to go alone, accompanied at most by one's dog—as long as he doesn't start chasing animals. When one is accompanied by other people, it is simply more difficult to open oneself up to the totality of unspoiled nature. A walk in the forest should serve to help one commune with and return to nature. Two people can just do it, but more than that—three, four or more people—makes it impossible for the forest to act upon one.

In addition, one can have other bad habits that interfere with an appreciation of nature. I remember that once my wife and I went from Seewiesen to a truly wonderful mixed forest nearby. There were incredibly beautiful song thrushes, large missle thrushes, wood warblers, and many more. Ours was a most beautiful springtime walk with the most marvelous sounds in the background. Suddenly, I heard a loudspeaker blaring rock music. A fifteen- or sixteen-year-old boy on a bicycle was riding over the crest of a hill on the forest path, with his radio blasting hellishly.

My wife said, "He's afraid that he might hear the birds singing." This facetious remark points to something very serious: There are too many people who, because of a lack of aesthetic education, consider pop music, shocking colors, and certain highly questionable modern art forms the *dernier cri* of creation. To them, the harmony of nature, of a forest, is not only not very attractive but downright repulsive. I have the vague feeling that they are aware of the inferiority of their own decadent aesthetic ideals but don't want to hear that there are harmonies other than those of electronics and computer games.

Uncontrolled dumps—which are sometimes more frequent today than anthills—should be outlawed. That's true not only in Austria but also in Bavaria. For example, not far from my institute in Bavaria there is a beautiful strip of forest. To the south, the dump borders on fields; from it, one can see the Zugspitze and the entire chain of the Alps. Precisely at that point, there lies an uncontrolled dump. That's really sad. It's not just that it's ugly: Many uncontrolled dumps in forests are poisonous time bombs that can endanger life, usually because of their influence on groundwater. It doesn't help for the media—radio and television stations and newspapers—to decry the existence of an uncontrolled dump if the wells in the next town are already contaminated and the people who drink the contaminated water end up in the hospital with painfully swollen stomachs. The danger of this type of damage is that one doesn't recognize it immediately. When one finally realizes that the groundwater is poisoned, then it's already too late. Preventive measures are needed to protect us in the future, but it will not be easy to institute them. Fortunately, most of the forests are not very accessible to big cities, so that one may at least hope that no huge dumps will arise in the forests.

*So much for people's lack of understanding about forests. What should everyone know about forests?*

I would say that the essential thing is to have a correct appreciation of the harmony of a forest. I think that one can probably better instill that in children by emotional means rather than by an exact, rational, biological education. What everyone should know about the forest is that in a living community, all creatures—animals, plants, and bacteria—depend on one another and the system can function only in an equilibrium.

We were just talking about unpleasant folktales with evil trolls in the forest and so forth. There are, however, happy folktales. Karl Ewald wrote a marvelous tale about the forest: Various creatures—both plants and animals—were discussing which of them was, in fact, the forest. First the beech tree said, "I'm the forest". Then the moss said, "You wouldn't be without me." The moss finally concluded that it was indispensable and said, "I am the forest." All the other creatures continued in the same way and at the end, the worm shouted, "I'm the forest," because without it, there would be no humus. The wisdom of this folktale, which one must teach to young and old, is this: There is no one creature that constitutes the forest; it's an interrelationship of a great number of completely different plants, animals, and bacteria. As I said, I think that one can understand this fact emotionally more easily than intellectually because, ecologically speaking, it's a fairly complex matter, a fairly complex, interlocking system. That's exactly why I think that it's important to create picture books with good, natural photographs of the forest. My young friend and interviewer Kurt Mündl has already made such books and these have helped to facilitate the preservation of nature. One must address the public at large, for only then does the sympathetic politician have the power to push through measures to protect the environment. Rather than advocating the formal study of ecology, one can teach people more effectively by encouraging them to walk in the forest, by giving picture books to their children, and by speaking to their emotions.

Unfortunately, a walk in the forest today is unsettling for a person who has lived a long time and who understands ecology. One forest that I know is so cleared and chopped down that its ecology has changed significantly. There are places where, in my youth, only thick moss grew for kilometers. Now ribbon grass grows there because there is too much light for moss, due to the thinning out of the forest. However, as we know, ribbon grass doesn't retain water as well as moss.

Forests that are still unspoiled in this respect are marvelous. One can see clearly how the trees and the ground cover live symbiotically, how the moss retains the water and that the largest, finest beeches grow exactly on those spots.

For someone like me, who has the advantage of long periods of observation, it is often frightening to go into a forest that seems to have no soul but, rather, a crude imitation made by man—a monoculture forest.

Given such development, I don't know how much longer there will be natural forests. No one knows that. It is absolutely impossible to forecast this because the results cannot be foreseen; as Karl Popper has shown, even an entire host of mechanisms that forecast and project cannot provide a truly reliable forecast about any future event. However, it is a truly frightening thought, for example, to imagine that all Christmas trees might be made of plastic one day, because I just now am trimming a beautiful Christmas tree. It occurred to me that it's really a sin these days to cut down a fir tree that is growing well. That's why I sympathize with people who use potted trees for Christmas and then plant them in their gardens after the holidays.

I think that it is particularly dangerous to substitute artificial things for natural ones. The lie implicit in accepting a plastic object as a fir tree is, in my opinion, highly demoralizing for children. One cannot lie to children about such things. It is by no means impossible that one day chopping down spruce and fir trees will be outlawed because there are too few of them. It is unbelievable how one clings to the customs of one's youth. In my case, this is even stronger because I live in the house where I lived as a child. The Christmas tree stands in its customary place and is trimmed with ornaments that my brother, who died ten years ago at the age of eighty-five, received as gifts when he was a child.

Before one robs someone of his traditional beliefs—which is something one shouldn't do at all—one should examine one's own soul to determine to what traditions one clings. A Christmas tree is an absolutely indispensable custom. Christmas without a Christmas tree would be horrible. I hope that I never live to see that day.

*One final question: Apocalypse? Central Europe without forests?*

I probably can imagine that the mountains will one day become karstic, the hills, too. One cannot imagine that when the forest is gone, the soil will remain on rounded mountains like those of the Viennese forest. The rain would flow right into the streams; none of it would remain on the peaks. Everything on the summits would dry up and there would be frightening floods after a downpour. I see this already in the stream in our village. Since there is too little moss in the forests, the thunderstorms cause the little stream to overflow, which is a great annoyance. One cannot imagine all that would happen if the water system was to go awry.

One must remember that the deserts—all deserts—bordering on farmland are spreading out at a tremendous rate every year; for example, north and south of the Sahara or in Texas. There where half a lifetime ago cotton grew—a plant that needs fairly good soil—there is now a sandy desert with shifting dunes. This transformation into steppes would probably be the fate of Central Europe or of all of Europe if the forest and the vegetation that retains water were to disappear.

One can say without a doubt and without any exaggeration that the desert follows the forest. One sees it wherever there is karst; for example, where the Venetians chopped down forests to build ships in olden times. When you look at the knolls of the hills at an angle, they look green; when you look at them straight ahead, however, they look gray because the blades of grass are so far apart from one another. The karstic and non-karstic regions along the Adriatic, the Mediterranean, and in Sardinia provide an object lesson in what happens when the forest disappears. It makes absolutely no difference whether you chop it down or eliminate it with acid rain.

That which follows the collapse of an ecosystem is always much poorer. This, too, is illustrated by the example of karst, for karst isn't dead. Plants grow there and wall lizards run across the stones. It would remain a habitat even after the forest was gone, but there's nothing there on which man could live.

Areas of karst can be used by people only to tend sheep and goats that graze from one blade of grass to another and that eat sparingly. However, the number of sheep that can live on a square kilometer of karst is only a fraction of that which can feed on a normal meadow.

Once again, to make it clear to people: Complete unemployment would be the result of the disappearance of the forest in Central Europe or Europe as a whole. Where hundreds of foresters and farmers once found their livelihood, perhaps only one family of shepherds would be able to live.

# ON THE DEATH OF
# THE WATERS

*P* *ollution is one of the problems of our time that knows no*
*boundaries. In the East as well as in the West, there is an*
*unspoken consensus that man has the right to arbitrarily*
*destroy the environment. A global example is the devastation of the*
*waters.*

Pollution of the waters is global suicide, particularly because
we don't yet realize what we are polluting, poisoning, and
destroying. Water is $H_2O$. One can produce it by oxidizing
hydrogen. A body of water, however, is not merely $H_2O$ but
a combination of many, many elements, of an endless number
of living beings that coexist in this body of water. It is a unity
dominated by an equilibrium between the animals, plants, and
bacteria, only the sum of which can be considered a body of
water. This balance can be disturbed very, very easily.

Today, unfortunately, we are all too often satisfied with
purifying sewage to obtain drinking water. This is a process
that is both dangerous and expensive. It is a tremendous error
to think that there are unlimited quantities of water and air at
our disposal. Many people who grow up in a city, who have

an enviable—or a damnable—confidence in technology, think this. They think that if only there was sufficient money, man could, produce everything, including water and air.

Mankind can destroy itself very easily with this error in thought. Once again, it is the powerful people of this world, the politicians and industrialists, who should try to prevent the approach of this tremendous catastrophe. There should be international preparedness and a willingness to discuss the ways of preserving those bodies of water—already many are almost hopelessly polluted—that are still healthy. Why doesn't that take place? Nothing better occurs to me than my old story; namely that the powerful and the rich are not so unethical as to let their own children and grandchildren die of thirst when all of the waters are irreparably polluted, but they simply don't believe that such a danger is real—just as they don't realize the dangers of nuclear power, of the chemical industry, of the death of forests, and so on.

The concept of reality has changed: Man considers something to be real only when it bears on his life directly, on an everyday basis. Therefore, those who are responsible for what happens in our environment simply don't realize, or else don't believe, that the dangers are as close, as oppressive, and as threatening as they are.

When we disturb the equilibrium of a body of water, we are doing something that cannot necessarily be undone. Naturally, when one stops poisoning a body of water it will, in time, return to a state of equilibrium. It is similar to what occurs in an aquarium where all the fish have died and the water is temporarily murky. In time, the water becomes clear again and the equilibrium is restored. However, this new equilibrium is not the same as that which preceded it. It is much poorer in the number of elements that comprise it and one cannot say that it is more stable just because it is composed of more resistant species whose equilibrium cannot be disturbed as easily. On the contrary, the stability of an ecosystem—and a body of water is an ecosystem—is proportional to the number of species that inhabit it. We must make the public aware of the irreversible and irrevocable nature of the pollution of the waters. If we kill a body of water, a body of water as a living system, a system that consists of many species, then we can never make up for this fully.

Thus the biocenosis becomes poorer and poorer, and it is erroneous to think that man alone will be impervious to this impoverishment and that he alone will survive when all other creatures perish. For this reason, the destruction of a body of water, the murder of a river or a lake, is always a step toward the suicide of humanity.

The foregoing reveals how a body of water dies and that it is, as a whole, mortal, which many people consider impossible. Can a lake, a river, a sea die like a person? The answer is a clear and unequivocal yes—with ten exclamation marks. A body of water dies in step-by-step catastrophes. The first creatures affected are of course the fish. Fish, which are highly developed animals that breathe water, are particularly sensitive to poisons. Therefore, when the Krems Chemie Company disgorges its pollution in the middle of the summer when the water level is low, then fish die, especially certain particularly sensitive species. And—the analogy is striking—just as acid rain primarily endangers tall trees, so large fish, especially females, die first.

A few years ago, when I still used to take walks regularly along the Danube, that part of the river that was nearest to where I lived was still unspoiled. It had not yet been destroyed by the Greifenstein dam. Since then, I have avoided the Danube for egotistical reasons; it depresses me too much. However, even then, the Krems Chemie Company began to kill fish. The first to die were usually barbels. Then the constant waves of pollution gradually changed the relation between the species: Certain types disappeared completely or were replaced by others that were more resistant. In the Danube, for example, during the course of my long life and before the dam was built—the Miller's thumb or *Mühlkoppe* as it is called in German—*Cottus gobio* has been replaced slowly, due to pollution and poison, by another type of Gobioid that migrated from the lower regions of the Danube. This fish adapted in a similar manner: It is a ground fish with a reduced swimming bladder, heavier than water, which supports itself on its fins. All Gobioids can do this because of a coadunation of their ventral fins. In all likelihood, this fish had gradually infiltrated the *cottus gobio* due to the change in the quality of the water. In any event, I suddenly noticed that the fish that I caught underneath the stones were no longer *cottus gobio* but the new ones. This isn't an easy thing to notice, even for an expert. In this way, species disappear and other species suddenly appear, which naturally indicates a significant change in the original equilibrium.

Those species that live closest to the surface of the river die and disappear. Since these fish need a great deal of oxygen, they are found where the water moves fastest.

The gradual disappearance of a species is characteristic of the death of a body of water. The number of species declines, whereas the number of individuals of a particular species often increases rapidly. For example, in waters that are becoming eutrophic, the migratory shell *dreissena polymorpha* frequently multiplies rapidly until there are colossal numbers of these creatures. This, in turn, is dangerous because overpopulation tends toward a collapse of the biological system. Such an occurrence has been seen in Lake Constance, where a huge overpopulation of *dreissena polymorpha* have developed on the south or Swiss side of the lake. I myself have witnessed the revolting stench of dying banks of *dreissena* when the water was low in Rorschach, on the south shore of Lake Constance. A partial catastrophe of a species that has multiplied beyond all bounds and then collapses destroys, of course, countless other creatures with it.

One can prove scientifically that an ecological system must consist of at least three elements; namely of plants, animals, and bacteria. Plants and animals form a symbiosis because plants produce oxygen that animals breathe and return to the plants as carbon dioxide, from which the plants produce by means of photosynthesis carbohydrates that are of value to animals. The third element in this union are bacteria, since plants and animals don't live forever. They must die, rot, and decompose into elements. That is the job of the bacteria. As you know, plants can assimilate; that means they can create organic matter from inorganic matter. This process, however, requires that bacteria decomposes dead matter so that it can be used again by green plants.

One cannot forget that when one of the elements of this triangle consisting of plants, animals, and bacteria disappears, then life is destroyed. This happens in extreme cases when plants or animals can no longer withstand the extreme change in their living conditions and die. This is followed by the stench of bacteria. You know the proverbial fatal clarity of dead bodies of water following such a change. Such bodies of water can even appear very beautiful. There are ponds in gravel pits that are completely dead because some poison got into them. They are so clear and the water appears so pure that one can see the bottom. Everyone thinks that the water is wonderful. In fact, the pond is, biologically speaking, a corpse, because the triangle plant-animal-bacteria is not in balance or because one element is lacking.

That is a short description of how a body of water can gradually die. It's bad enough when only one species is lacking in the original structure. A famous Austrian scientist once said, "Toads are dispensable, they don't matter." In fact, nothing is dispensable. The disappearance of every species of plant and animal diminishes the stability of the ecological system and brings us closer to the death of the environment, a death that man as a member and participant in the environment cannot escape.

The Danube and the Rhine, which today lie in a coma, are examples, sad examples. Both rivers are threatened by immediate extinction.

The media has written a lot about these rivers, so I will only talk about my own observations, about that which I personally have learned and experienced. I know one of the tributaries of the Rhine very well: the Neckar. My son and my grandchildren lived near this river for years. There was a time when detergents, which reduce the surface tension of water, polluted the Neckar to such a degree that mountains of foam many meters high formed on weirs, small waterfalls, and sluices. I took a walk along the Neckar with my family in Heidelberg. While we were looking at the shocking towers of foam, we found a river crab lying on the bank, out of the water. It had bailed out because the water was so foul. Imagine, this aquatic creature preferred to live on the dry bank. Just imagine!

We took the crab home and my grandson Bertram, who likes aquariums, kept him; he lived for years in tap water, which is somewhat better than river water. The crab lacked nothing. It wasn't the animal that was sick but, rather, the Neckar.

With an aquarium, one can teach every child how a body of water can die. Ideally, an aquarium is an environment that maintains itself, where plants, animals, and bacteria coexist in equilibrium. Naturally, one must take certain steps to preserve this equilibrium, since if you put three fish in the tank, then you have to feed them and then change the water to compensate for the disruption of the autonomy of this little body of water. Nevertheless, one can learn very well what conditions a body of water needs in order to survive.

Let's turn to the general fact that one can poison a large river with chemicals: It was only a relatively short time ago that we realized that one can't release all of the wastes of a paper mill into a river without killing it.

In the Middle Ages, salmon mounted the Rhine all the way to Basel, to the headwaters of the Rhine. Salmon were so common then that there was a law that forbade estate owners from giving workers and peasants salmon more than twice a week. Today this superb fish is one of the most expensive delicacies in the world. This alone shows the changes that have occurred over the course of time in the fauna of the major rivers of Central Europe. However, one can say with certainty that in no other century has the ecology of the rivers been so seriously altered and damaged as in our own. It is a sad fact that our society requires so much time to learn from its mistakes and to act judiciously. Unfortunately, nature doesn't have so much time; it is sensitive and reacts abruptly to change, as the Rhine and Danube have demonstrated.

One must know, among other things, that still waters belong to a river's ecological system—the still waters or tributaries are linked to the river itself. Many types of fish spawn in these still waters. In addition, very few plants grow in the river itself because of the flowing current. The plant performs its job—an indispensable one in the ecological system—primarily in the still waters. I recently heard that only about two percent of the original calm waters of the Danube are still connected to the river. That means that the changes in the river, which were accomplished to aid shipping, cut the river off from its still waters, robbed the fish of their preferred spawning grounds, and deprived the river of the activities of green plants that take place to a great degree in the still waters and that are necessary for the functioning of the entire system.

When a river is channeled, one has only to diminish the calm waters in order to lower the water level, because the river digs deeper into its bed. If, in addition, the banks of the river are covered with impermeable materials, then the water table faces a catastrophe that, in the case of the Rhine, has already assumed major proportions. Industry begins to fight for its rights and the groups that are interested in a channeled river that is cut off from its meadows are probably financially stronger than the hunters and fishermen who probably prefer having meadows lie next to the quiet arms of the river.

Embedding rivers in concrete coffins is one of the saddest aspects of the disfiguration and ruin of the landscape that one can imagine. It is a frightening consequence of the erroneous thinking of modern people, engineers, landscape planners, and even completely average property owners.

I recall, albeit not with pleasure, a discussion that I had with some people who want order. It was an unusual case in which Professor Lötsch was involved. He arranged the discussion centered around straightening the course of a small brook. Straightening this small brook would have resulted in a decline in the level of the water table, which would not have improved but worsened the meadows along the brook. The first question that we posed to the advocate of this measure was why he wanted to do it. The man provided several reasons why it would be desirable to straighten the course of the brook. We were able biologically and ecologically to explain and refute all of the reasons. Therefore, we saw no reason why the little brook should not be left as it was. Finally, when the poor fellow was at a loss for arguments to support his position, he said, "But it's much more beautiful when it is a straight streamlet in concrete than a twisting brook!" The man was, of course, beyond help. One's despair at hearing such a thing is really heartrending.

An impermeable strengthening of a river's bank is death, of course, because the river loses contact with the shallows, the little pools and all the marshes near its banks that are vital for it to function. Man's creativity is boundless, however, when it comes to doing things badly. The straight bed of a brook encased in concrete is not the worst crime. The bed of the brook encased in concrete is still one degree better than putting the entire brook in pipes and placing them under the surface of the earth. That is a favorite solution. Such a solution is, of course, the unconditional end for a body of water. When one sees what is gained by this artificial stagnation—an entirely minimal gain compared with the gigantic losses for the entire world—one is speechless at how stupid mankind can be. The collective stupidity of man is incredible.

To a certain extent, one repeats oneself when one talks about the destruction of all types of water. What is the point of this straightening, putting brooks in pipes, other than perverse aesthetic considerations? The response is that what is sought is only the efficient use of the immediate surroundings. This brings us inevitably to the question of meadows. The danger posed by the construction of dams and all the accompanying threats—most of which have been discussed previously—lie in the fact that no one is interested in providing the lowlands, which are cut off from the river by the impermeable embankment, with sufficient water. The exception is the conservationist, who knows how important an unspoiled ecological system is for the surroundings far and near.

Most of the people who live near a river, not only industrialists but also farmers, want dry meadows. Dry meadows already exist in part: The Danube meadows have become much drier during my own lifetime. Just the taming of the river in about 1870 caused the still waters to fill up with sedimentation to such a degree that bodies of water that were navigable at an average water level during my student days are no longer navigable. The hollow areas eroded by the river, which contained enough water to paddle on in my youth, are now completely dried up and overgrown. My wife and I called such a hollow a wadi, because even then they dried up when there was no rain for a long time. Today they are so overgrown that one can barely find them.

In the fishing area at Wördern, there are two artesian springs where the water emerges from deep underground. I'm curious to know what these springs will do when the water table rises. I hope that they will be revitalized, but it all depends on where the water comes from. Otherwise, a literal devastation by drought will result from creating an impermeable embankment.

There are high areas in the original meadow—interesting regions at that—dry zones or hot moors. Strangely enough, there you find pines and sea buckthorns growing in the middle of the Danube meadow. In all likelihood, these dry areas of the lowlands, which arose because of insufficient water, will spread even though they are quite rare. In essence, that's a natural process but it means that the true character of the lowlands will be lost. It would be good if at least small areas—for example, the left bank above the Greifenstein dam, where there are still wonderful lowlands—would remain unspoiled. However, it's not good if they are too small and insulated. There are reasons why a certain size is desirable, because the number of different creatures declines with a decrease in the amount of space available. However, one could counteract this drying up, at least locally. One of the duties of Austrian conservationists should be to provide sufficient funds—the sum would have to be a fixed amount in the budget—to maintain the moisture level of certain meadows. That must be attainable.

It is more difficult to defend the right of the damp and acidic meadows to survive. Agricultural and economic interests are too much in the fore. I think that it is hard to explain to a farmer that he shouldn't drain a damp meadow because storks find their food and food for their young there in the spring and summer, or because the lapwing needs an appropriate breeding ground. I must say it's harder to blame a farmer who wants to turn his property into farmland and grow grain than it is to blame a chemical company that wants to construct a building on what it perceives as a worthless damp meadow.

The farmer at least still has a good understanding of the process of life that occurs during the cycle of the seasons. He knows when he should sow, plow, and harvest. He also knows that he must return something to nature if he has only plundered it for years. Seen from this perspective, one is better able to appreciate the farmer's lack of understanding when he wants to transform worthless land—a damp, acidic meadow—into farmland. In this case, there is still a direct relationship between the act and the benefit. However, I consider it a crime when a mayor drains a damp meadow where rare orchids grow only to construct a municipal dump or tennis courts.

In this respect, too, one must admit that the Danube and the Rhine are almost dead. Perhaps this is more true of the Rhine; whereas the Danube, by comparison, is not in such a dire state. The Danube still flows uncontrolled in certain stretches. These natural locations should be maintained at all costs because they contain their own fauna. The reservoirs that are dammed up, however, are peculiarly lacking in plant and animal life because the water doesn't flow there anymore. Reservoirs are so deep and their banks so steep that hardly any plants can flourish. Professor Wendelberger told me that one finds very few plants in reservoirs. Of course, little by little, plants and animals that grow in still water spread, but it takes years for them to flourish.

In short, the reservoir itself is deficient in life. The sight of waterfowl does not necessarily mean the system is healthy. Ducks are evident there because they prefer still water. Although everything appears very natural, in reality the dam is biologically and ecologically quite moribund. This is especially true when smaller rivers are dammed, resulting in periodic strong rises and falls in the water level. When the water level rises and falls significantly, normal vegetation cannot take root on the banks. The marsh zone, which permits many kinds of plants and animals in a river to survive, disappears. The dam at Enns, where Professor Koenig founded an ecological institute, suffers greatly from such shifting water levels.

One has to remember that there are no tides in freshwater as there are in the sea. For this very reason, there are, of course, no organisms that are adapted to tides and can endure the constantly changing ebb and flow, a situation that is artificially produced in some dams.

The Rhine is in much worse shape than the Danube because the latter is much less polluted. From Basel onward, there are large factories situated along the Rhine that pollute the river with their waste. Whereas on the Danube, there are large factories only from Linz onward. There is still life in and along the Danube that could be saved. In short, one can say that the Rhine is dead and that the Danube is in its death throes.

Perhaps even more dramatic than the condition of large bodies of water is the general state of pools and ponds. A pond, which for decades or even centuries was the breeding pool for frogs and toads, can be ruined when a driver throws a used car battery into it.

Someone who lived amid nature when young now must miss the symphony of the frogs, the sonorous concert of toads after the Danube had flooded its banks. One really could help animals so that their population does not dwindle to extinction. In such cases, one could actually supply "secondhand nature."

With only a few artificial spawning grounds, one could prevent animals from dying out in a particular area. Even today, there is nothing more exciting than to make a small pond in one's garden.

Of course, such measures make sense only when one educates the public at large. One must keep people from dumping filth into the artificial pools—especially car batteries. Because of the acid and heavy metals in car batteries, they are the most poisonous things that one can throw into a small body of water. A pool where a car battery has been thrown is usually destroyed forever. Pools are usually fed by groundwater and not by the current of a stream and therefore water is exchanged must too slowly for a pool to regenerate itself. Secondly, the maxim that applies to every aquarium applies here; namely that the smaller a body of water is, the harder it is to maintain its equilibrium. Some pools in the forest measure only few square meters. Nevertheless, they are essential for a highly complex biological community. The disposal of unpleasant garbage is the main cause of the sorry state of so many pools and ponds. A second destructive factor is that so many pools have been filled with soil. A pool often is considered undesirable because it might be used more effectively as a vegetable patch, and because mosquitoes breed in many pools. Up until a few years ago, it was common to pour petroleum into a forest pool. The petroleum did indeed destroy the mosquito larvae because the petroleum spread across the surface of the pool. The larvae couldn't penetrate the petroleum layer with their breathing pipes and so they were deprived of fresh air. Since larvae don't breathe through gills underwater but need fresh air from above the water, they died.

However, in addition, all of the natural enemies of the mosquitoes were killed also. These included all the organisms that live in pools and eat mosquitoes: newts, dragonfly larvae, water bugs, and Nepidae. The first creatures that recolonize an impoverished pool are the mosquitoes. They are specialists at it. They fly better than the other insects and arrive first. Mosquito larvae can flourish in the puddles left on a mud path by vehicle tires—as long as the puddles don't dry out too fast. The problem is that the mosquito's natural enemies, whose time span between generations is not as short, had been eliminated for a long, long time, with the result that the mosquitoes could multiply more than ever before because man stupidly and shortsightedly intervened in the natural order. This is a disagreeable fact that easily can be applied to other human actions, with equally catastrophic results.

Throughout my life, the pools from which I took food for my aquariums have all been destroyed by old cars and other poisonous things.

There is a very good book entitled *Rettet die Frösche* by Thielcke, Herrn, Hutter, and Schreiber.* Even before I read this book, I am proud to say that I already had taken measures—and rather expensive measures at that—to save my frogs. First I put out a small swimming pool with unfiltered water in which the tree frogs could spawn. Unfortunately, it didn't work out as I had hoped: Not all of the tadpoles hatched and only a few developed completely into frogs. To improve the results, I spent a good deal of money on a big natural pond in my garden—using a plastic sheet to trap the water—as an appropriate breeding ground for tree frogs. On the one hand, it helps the frogs, while on the other, it gives me the pleasure of hearing the tree frog concert in the garden.

A tree frog, *Hyla arborea*, lives a very long time, like most other amphibians. That's why one observes that in regions where no tree frogs have reproduced for six or seven years because all of all the polluted pools, one can still occasionally hear the "singing" of tree frogs. Whoever wants to start a frog pond—an enterprise that is very laudable—can try, of course, to add frog eggs or tadpoles. However, this only works when there are meadows, trees, and bushes around the pond where the adult frogs can look for food. Before beginning such a project, one should talk with conservationists or experts, since in some countries not only the adult frogs but even the eggs

*In English, Save the Frogs.

and the tadpoles are protected. Moreover, the inexperienced person occasionally can cause more harm than good. This is comparable to feeding birds during the winter: More birds die because of incorrect feeding than would naturally die during a normal winter without extremely low temperatures. One either can wait until the frogs come of their own accord and accept the pond as a spawning ground or else add eggs, which is not without risks from the point of view of conservation. The one thing that doesn't work is putting adult frogs in the pond. They will simply return to their spawning grounds, unless, of course, they've voluntarily chosen the newly created pond.

I have gotten a great deal of pleasure from the ordinary swimming pool that I purchased. Aside from my attempts to get tree frogs to spawn there, two varieties of dragonflies have hatched and grown to maturity there. This was fraught with difficulties, since dragonflies that have just hatched need a ladder in the form of reeds and the like. The dragonfly larvae crawl out of the water, and only then does the insect hatch. In a swimming pool, the possibility of climbing up is very limited. However, next year the situation will be remedied, for I now have a pond sixteen meters in diameter with flat banks and swamp plants, and therefore climbing should no longer be a problem. The pond was finished this autumn, but we cannot put water in it until next spring. I hope that dragonflies and perhaps even tree frogs will accept it during the first year. Aside from my pond, however, all of the ponds within a day's walk of Altenberg have been destroyed, all ponds in which once upon a time one could have caught daphnia and fish food. A few new Danube ponds have appeared near the flood dams, and these may prove viable and even able to support colonization by new creatures. It is, above all, a question of time.

Nevertheless, one must realize that all of the waters and habitats that are closely connected to the water supply and that are influenced and destroyed by man are subject to a great variety of dangers. It is not always so easy to determine who is guilty of destruction. The desolate state of the waters in lakes, for example, can be caused by hotels. Lake Millstätt was saved at the last minute by a circular sewer. I once saw Lake Zürich in a truly desolate state, whereas now it is completely all right because the Swiss are active conservationists. Presently, one can see the quality, the purity of the water by the number of waterfowl that can live there again.

As far as lakes are concerned, I would say that the primary polluters are hotels and private individuals who live along the shore and who release sewage and washing water into the lake. In the case of rivers, I would say industry is the primary culprit. A paper mill can wreak frightful damage, as, of course, can all the other factories that release chemical waste into a river. There are, therefore, a great variety of pests, human pests, which all play a role. However, it's not enough just to complain, one must explain which measures will stop the damage. A circular sewer is certainly a superb solution to save a lake. On the other hand, one must bear in mind that even though the discharge of the circular sewer doesn't directly damage the lake, the polluted water doesn't evaporate. Therefore, if there is no complicated sewage-treatment plant, a circular sewer is no solution.

If I am compelled to prognosticate—something that I do not like to do and that I do only with certain provisos—then I would have to say that things will have to get much worse before they get better. There must be a turning point, because otherwise mankind has had it. The big question is *when* the turning point will occur. In some cases, one can, of course, take the offensive in preventing the further destruction of nature instead of remaining on the defensive. One can take measures to restore and heal what has been damaged, although it is always better to preserve the natural state. Occasionally, the restoration of natural conditions is indeed promising. I recently read an article in an American newspaper about how the Hudson River was saved. The Hudson was so polluted that it once actually caught on fire. As a popular song goes: "The Danube fell into the water, the ice has burnt up. St. Stephen's belfry has gone mad and run to put it out." Of course, it wasn't the river itself that caught fire but, rather, the surface, which was totally polluted with an oil slick. Although the Americans are the worst sinners in this respect, they are always the first to take corrective measures. However, since the years of the Reagan administration, this praise may be a bit hasty. In any event, after strict conservation and environmental laws were passed to preserve the Hudson, the river returned to health again and now is used by fish to spawn. The proof of this is seen in the huge sturgeon that are caught near Albany; they can't swim farther upstream because there's a waterfall.

Therefore the Hudson and Lake Millstätt are examples of the fact that one can, within limits, repair the damage that has been done. I emphasize *within limits.*

The situation is completely different as far as the sea is concerned.

This is where I must really get up on my soapbox and warn people very urgently. I do this not because I study sea animals but because my warning is general and concerns all of humanity; namely that one cannot restore oceans. Once an ocean has died, it is dead; one can do what one wants, but when marine species have died, when they are extinct, they cannot be re-created.

I have seen tremendous damage done to the oceans by fertilizers. Marine organisms are much less adaptable than freshwater creatures. When, for example, in Hawaii, the sugar-beet fields are fertilized and strong rains wash the fertilizer into the ocean, all sorts of things can happen. One result can be a red tide. This occurs as a result of a sudden, incredible increase in the number of flagellants, which withdraw so much oxygen from the water that the other organisms that require oxygen die. This causes entire reefs to die, reefs where coral was clearly growing just a year before, far into the open sea. Thereafter, the reef is dead and overgrown by green algae. These green algae are *poisonous.* Fish that eat plants come and eat these algae and then retain the poisons in their bodies. Fish that feed on other fish rather than plants eat these fish and retain the poison in their bodies, which are themselves now so poisonous that a human would die immediately if one ate a fish caught near a reef. The barracuda, *Sphyraena barracuda*, for example, is considered poisonous on certain coasts of Hawaii, whereas in Florida, where there are no fertilized fields near the ocean, one can eat it without worrying.

On the whole, I consider oil less destructive than detergents. I have seen oil leak out on seawater aquariums and nothing has happened. We sucked up the oil by blotting paper and the aquariums did not "tip over" ecologically. Of course, this isn't necessarily comparable to a catastrophe where oil spreads over many square kilometers of the ocean. Nevertheless, aquatic life would be more endangered if many people washed themselves with soap in the ocean than it is from oil. My experience with saltwater aquariums has shown that an oil spill is catastrophic for waterfowl, seals, and all the other animals that must surface to breathe; but it is less harmful to the creatures that live underwater than other types of pollution. I didn't say harmless, I said less harmful.

The few cases where bodies of water have actually been rehabilitated give grounds for optimism. However, it's difficult to say whether or not first aid will arrive in time and before the point of no return is reached. Many believe it will, and I still hope it will.

I wouldn't preach so insistently about ocean systems as I do if I was not so well informed, better informed than the average zoologist. I know how vulnerable seawater and all of the organisms that live in it are. My great fear is that the oceans as a whole will collapse as they have in certain places.

The Mediterranean is literally on the brink of "tipping over." Fortunately, however, completely ludicrous factors may help to save it. For example, there is tourism. Tourists on the Adriatic coast are offended because the water stinks, and that ironically helps save the Adriatic.

We must realize that the ocean does not exist for us just to swim in, or so that we can sail around in yachts. The ocean is essential for the survival of all of us. Mankind doesn't pay attention to such things. The laments about our dying forests may create the hope that people's attitudes are changing; but catastrophes can affect the entire ocean at any time, and then we will suffocate, because the oxygen we breathe is created to a large extent by sea algae.

Apart from these international dangers, in particular the danger of the destruction of the oceans, I am a patriot who defends what is nearby. My concern at the moment are the pools of water.

I felt obliged to put a pond in my garden to help the tree frogs. However, many people don't understand this; such values are foreign to them. If the system being destroyed was synthetic or man-made, they would be able to understand such an act more easily. However, they can't understand that wiping out a species or an entire ecosystem is just as undermining and probably more unethical than destroying a cathedral, a venerable old edifice. At least, with the pond in my garden I hope that during my own lifetime I can send a few thousand tree frogs out into the world.

# CONSERVATION, PROTECTING ANIMALS, EXPERIMENTING ON ANIMALS

*E*veryone talks about conservation today. Aside from the fact that conservation can have both positive and negative effects, I would like to ask whether conservation is at all possible in areas frequented by people or whether nature can only be protected in completely isolated areas.

It is certainly a poor solution to bar people from seeing natural, harmonious landscapes, because they should know and appreciate how beautiful unspoiled nature is and can be. For that reason, it's desirable to reach a synthesis wherever possible between the requirements of conservation on the one hand and people's need to experience nature on the other. If one is clever about it, it is indeed possible to combine conservation and tourism, for example. It is indeed possible to reconcile animals—especially birds—with tourism as long as there is *no shooting,* because then the animals become half-tame.

In the Florida Everglades, a huge swamp, there are paths for tourists—wooden docks on stilts—that lead into mangrove areas. From there, one can look only a few meters away into the nests of snakebirds, herons, and cormorants. The brooding birds are not bothered at all because they know from experience that the people passing by can't get any closer than the path permits and that no one will jump into the water—if only because of the alligators—to rob the nests. The inbred fear of man has been largely eliminated because hunting is forbidden—no one can shoot there. After all, one can't expect a bird to brood near a path from which people shoot.

That's the way it is in the Everglades, and it's a good example of how one should approach the matter. The situation shows that the money spent by tourists doesn't have to be at the expense of nature. Nevertheless, this sort of thing works only when the tourism is controlled, when there is no shooting and no one leaving the path. Unfortunately, there are a lot of examples of how not to do it.

Along the Danube, between Muckendorf and Greifenstein, there were colonies of terns living on the bare gravel banks until shortly before the Second World War. Common terns and even little terns lived there. On certain arms of the Stockerau where some foliage grew, there were even *Trauerseeschwalben*. All of these terns and colonies of other birds didn't die from poisoning or shooting but, rather, from tourism.

Seemingly innocuous actions can, in fact, be quite harmful. For example, one lovesick couple may jeopardize the existence of a tern colony by landing a rowboat on one of the terns' islands, spending a hot summer day relaxing, while being oblivious to the terns, who are afraid to land on the ground. The lovers, of course, think nothing is amiss, because the untrained eye and ear don't notice the birds' nests on the ground or hear the "tierr, tierr, tierr," the warning cry of the terns wheeling in the air. They don't understand that they should leave so that the birds can return to their brood or to feeding their young. A few holidays with tourists in rowboats are enough to destroy the colonies of terns. Uncontrolled tourism can cause unbelievable damage in ecologically and biologically valuable regions—which today means practically everywhere.

Needless to say, the tourists' destruction of the terns was unintentional; the terns died through lack of understanding.

However, precisely the opposite does occur: A natural environment can be destroyed for commercial reasons in the service of tourism. A good example of this are the reeds along the banks of lakes. I'm thinking specifically of the Neusiedler Lake, whose reedy banks offer an immense protection for all sorts of creatures. For many of these creatures, a band of reeds along a lake is vital for survival. Swimmers, however, do not like reeds along the bank of a lake. The mayors of the towns situated on lakes are, of course, in favor of eliminating the reeds to create a sandy beach, and are even more in favor of it if someone wants to build a hotel. I remember the spectacular trial of my journalist friend Graupe. He so vehemently attacked a hotel operator who was illegally building a hotel that the hotel operator brought suit against him. My friend Otto Koenig and I testified correctly and truthfully against the hotel operator, since people frequently don't understand what damage uncontrolled tourism can cause to flora and fauna.

However, conservation can assume strange forms, so that one sometimes asks what the word *conservation* means. Take fishing, for example. In America and England, there are undoubtedly a lot of fishermen who love nature and who are conservationists. Nevertheless, in these countries, it is not at all common to slaughter a fish when it is caught. One fish after another is caught and tossed into the boat, where it dies a slow and cruel death by suffocation. Here is a case where a sense of pity, of conservation, of kindness to animals fails to exist because these people were not taught such sensibilities in their earliest childhood.

It is easy to teach children respect for living creatures and ecological systems. Take a child, a ten-year-old boy, who unfortunately must grow up in an apartment in the city. You can teach him about conservation very easily if you enable him to come into contact with animals. An aquarium and a bird in a cage are superb teaching aids. As the child learns to be responsible for an animal, he will easily learn to shoulder responsibility for the environment as a whole.

It makes an incredible impression on children when they

receive a bird cage with two zebra finches that begin to brood and then suddenly six offspring appear. That's one way of teaching conservation to children in a big city. Nevertheless, even though a zebra finch in a bird cage is better than no animal at all—one should never forget that—still, it is not as good as a blackbird or a hawfinch on the windowsill of a birdhouse in the garden. That's why the best way to teach children about conservation is to take them out into the countryside. There's no better way to teach children distinctions. A child should know how beautiful a trout stream is compared to an industrial drainage ditch.

Take me as an example. I didn't turn to conservation or become a member of an organization; I was involved from the very beginning because I was born to it. I am thankful that I have always lived close to nature. However, my sense of conservation is derived in particular from the aquarium and the bird cage. I always had an aquarium and I always kept birds. Above all, I always collected wild animals in order to observe them. Oddly enough, there are two types of people who are interested in animals: The first are "farmers" and the second are "hunters."

I count myself among the "farmers," by which I mean animal lovers who enjoy nothing more than acquiring a new animal that is well, that eats heartily, and that may even reproduce in captivity. That's the ultimate pleasure.

The "hunter" is different. The hunter goes out into nature to observe animals without thinking of keeping and feeding them at home. Ideally, both types of animal lovers are able to be active conservationists. However, today's youth has more difficulty than did the youth of my day. This brings us to the double aspect of conservation. Here's an example: In my youth, I could go to a pool and catch frogs and tadpoles. Today, it's against the law to catch frogs in my country. If you take a frog from the meadow, you're breaking the law and could go to jail.

However, such laws have a negative side. Had I not been able to catch birds as a boy, I wouldn't be the specialist that I am today.

All too frequently these days, however, a mayor dries up a wet meadow to construct tennis courts. Then there is a ceremony. Medals are awarded and the ribbon across the entrance is cut with great festivity. Nobody notices how many frogs will be killed by the drying up of the meadow. A specific figure would not be representative because it would include only those frogs alive at the time, whereas if one considers the future, the number would much higher because it would include the unborn—due to the fact one is destroying the area where frogs breed every spring. People don't look at it that way, however.

Today, of course, it is of vital significance to protect many species. Entire biotopes overseas are being decimated by disreputable amateurs who capture animals and fish.

Anyone can be an active conservationist; just having a garden will suffice. Frogs have found a new spawning ground in the pond in my garden. Now, after two years, three varieties of frogs spawn there. With this simple form of conservation, I have allowed more frogs to breed than a person can eat.

The most important way to teach conservation to young people is to provide them a contact with animals. A child should be able to recall that when he was little, he had a terrarium, and that gradually fewer and fewer frogs were left in it, until one day there was only a gigantic garlic toad that had eaten all the others. That's how one learns.

In any event, the only way to educate adults is to teach them about conservation as children. Older people are too old to understand that. One should raise legions of conservationists in order to save our world.

The most important thing is a host of good teachers. Teachers have become objects of scorn, ludicrous figures, ever since Wilhelm Busch's* time, and that is very bad. The teacher should be elevated to an ideal position, because he can teach children in their earliest years what conservation is and what is at stake. Up until now, that has been very difficult. *An elementary school teacher should have the social status and the financial*

*A nineteenth-century German artist, author of popular children's books.*

*benefits of a university professor,* because the first teacher who instills an understanding of nature is exercising a very great influence. There are very few conservationists among the next generation because there are fewer and fewer adults devoted to nature. Fewer and fewer hours of the curriculum are directed to biology. Often biology has become the least important course in high school. People simply don't believe that they will be in dire straits in a hundred years because of their lack of understanding in this area. The situation is already very serious. Most little boys easily recognize a make of car—no matter how similar cars are, they can distinguish them perfectly—but don't know what kind of bird is flying past.

Aside from the family, which certainly can teach children to respect nature—to the extent that it's not blind to values—I see teachers who are ecologically trained as our greatest hope. It's the job of a good teacher to teach children the love of nature and to display in the right light the many great difficulties with which the world must grapple.

I had a marvelous biology teacher in high school and a brilliant one in elementary school. I don't know to which one I am most thankful. In general, I tend to feel the most thankful toward those who influenced my life in a positive way at the earliest stage.

Conservation and the protection of animals concern the teaching of values. I once proposed an experiment to prove that every human being possesses certain values. Imagine the following: I set up a long table on which there was a huge knife, a machete. On the table there was also a head of lettuce, a mussel, a salamander, a puppy, a baby chimpanzee, and a human baby. I put the machete into the hand of my human subject and told him to cleave one of these creatures in two with one blow. Anyone who did not pick the head of lettuce failed. Fortunately, almost all the people tested had the right sense of values.

One doubts human ethics when one sees how animals are kept in close quarters for the purpose of financial gain. I don't mean small farmers who have a personal contact with their

112

animals and who know them intimately and treat them well even though they may end up in the slaughterhouse. I do mean the production-line maintenance of animals, which is without a doubt one of the darkest and most shameful chapters in human culture. If you have ever stood before a stable where animals are being fattened and have heard hundreds of calves bleating, if you can understand the calf's cry for help, then you will have had enough of those people who derive profit from it.

I eat meat but rarely veal. It's natural to eat meat, but let's put it this way: If I had to slaughter the animals that I wanted to eat, I would certainly not eat beef. These are my own values. I could never bring myself to slaughter a cow. This is very difficult to do to any animal that one has taken care of for a long time.

Angelika Schlager, who put together in my home a very nice little aquarium with fish from this region, added, among other things, some roach eggs. Of course, the roaches that hatched grew larger and larger until they ate all of the plants in the aquarium. Naturally, Angelika could have fed them to larger fish, but she simply couldn't kill fish that she had known from the time they were small. That's completely normal. Every normal person would act in the same way. There's nothing particularly praiseworthy about it; it's just a normal reaction.

If one doesn't know what to do with the creatures one studies, then one doesn't have to kill them senselessly; one can eat them oneself, provided that one is able to do this. Take, for example, Jürg Lamprecht and his tilapia. Jüg Lamprecht works with cichlids, which are marvelous animals for experiments. However, many of those that he used became huge. Finally, he noticed that there simply wasn't room for such big animals in his limited aquarium. And so he said, "I'll eat them," which is just what he did. Gudrun had to cook them. In short, that wasn't a bad use for them.

Even today I am deeply indebted to dice snakes, water frogs, and laughing frogs. Among the prisoners of war in Russia, there were many with horrid edemas resulting from hunger and malnutrition, especially from a lack of proteins. I consumed numerous dice snakes and frogs in order to avoid that. One can't eat ring snakes because they smell so badly that it's absolutely impossible. Today, it wouldn't occur to me to eat frogs' legs or something similar because there are simply too few frogs and I would feel sorry for them. I have also eaten countless geese during my long life—gray geese—but I never slaughtered one. Whenever we had a roast goose, it was always the result of an accident. Even then I felt a certain reservation when carving the goose, and it was particularly difficult when I knew the goose well. As I said, there are certain values that hinder one. I can put it another way: Imagine we're on an expedition to the North Pole and find that food is running out. The members of the expedition confer and then say, "Let's roast old Konrad; after all, he's over eighty and can't do much any longer"—then I would be very offended. If I fell from a glacier and died, however, then I would say, "Please, help yourselves." It's purely a question of values.

Another question of values arises when one is forced to destroy animals for scientific reasons—for experiments, for example. This is a case where I am completely divided. It's much worse when someone's child dies than when a monkey that is kept in a cage dies. I consider it wrong to advocate banning all experiments on animals. A friend of mine, Monika Holzapfel, a great ethologist and biologist, lost her nine-year-old daughter, who died painfully from polio. One then must confront the question of how many baby rhesus monkeys must be tortured to death in order to save Monika Holzapfel's daughter? How many rhesus monkey lives are equal to that of one child? Such questions illustrate why it's completely insane to unequivocally prohibit large-scale tests on animals.

These questions are not easy to answer, however. Needless to say, I am against putting drops of nail polish into rabbits' eyes just to see what happens. Such research can be avoided. A decision is certainly easier to reach regarding unnecessary research such as this than it is concerning essential basic medical research with animals.

One should realize that in many ways an animal suffers not

less but more than we do. Once when I was on a trip, the root of my tooth became infected and I had nothing with me other than sleeping pills—no painkillers, just sleeping pills. I was stupid enough to take a sleeping pill. The pain was horrible, but normally one can cling to one's remaining fragments of reason in order to distract oneself from the pain. With the use of the sleeping pills, however, all semblance of reason was gone. With such a loss of reason, one is then hopelessly enslaved to the pain. With an animal, this is always the case.

A human can suffer without being sad: I was once on a Belgian ship crossing the English Channel. I was so seasick that I wanted to die. I was as physically sick as one can be, but I wasn't the least bit sad because I saw the pier of Ostende and knew that in fourteen minutes we would arrive and the horrible suffering would be over. Lacking such human perception, an animal can't reason in this way. When you go on vacation and leave your dog at home for two weeks, the dog suffers as much as if you had died because it's impossible for him to understand that you will return. Of course, when you merely go to work and return in the evening, the dog is trained to accept this because the time span is so short. He understands what is happening, and after a while, he knows not to take the absence so seriously. On the other hand, one should add that dogs forget quickly. Dogs forget people fairly quickly; in a decade, they can forget a person. A dog has a short life. Long-lived birds—ones that live sixty or seventy years as in the case with parrots and gray geese—have an unbelievable memory.

*Conservation not only concerns preserving individual species but entire biological systems. What are the pressing value questions that concern us here?*

In today's world, science unfortunately tries to quantify more and more, which is very bad. Money is guilty of everything. It has created an almost religious belief that natural systems can be evaluated, that so many square kilometers of forest are worth so many thousand dollars. This is a fundamental error. The entire forest is priceless, since when it's destroyed—destroyed forever—then it can't be had again for all the money in the world. People, including conservationists, must finally recognize the value of that which can't be recreated. A technical idiot might says, "Why should I protect the ibex? What I can make with technology is much more valuable." Not by a long shot! Such a person thinks that he could make a tree frog if only he had enough money, just as he can build a rocket for a certain sum. The point is that one can't do anything with species that are extinct; one can't even make a blade of grass when there is no more grass or seed.

Unfortunately, one cannot appeal to so-called logic, because logic is a system of various thought processes that developed during the course of mankind's prehistory and contributed to his cultural development. One cannot, unfortunately, develop a compelling argument on the basis of logic. The theoreticians of evolutionary cognition understand very well how differently existing objects impress themselves on our experience. We are not at all surprised when we encounter the same object one time as a stream of particles and another as a wave. It doesn't surprise me in the least when the same principle is true of our bodies and souls. When I say "My friend Kurt is sitting there," I certainly don't mean solely the physiological representation of your body, nor do I mean the singular presence of your soul. The fact is that you are a living being as I am and your presence there represents a combination of the body and spirit.

Therefore, one will definitely be unable to convince people that nature must be protected with logical arguments; one must explain it and look for examples. Otherwise, one can never convince people that nuclear power as such is bad, that it's a dead end of mankind's development in which one can become trapped, in which mankind can perish. Everywhere there are certain controls at work. A control system in which there is positive feedback is perforce in an imbalance, and there are only very few control systems in the realm of social interaction that are created to produce a negative feedback. Negative feedback occurs when the carburetor is full; then the float stops the flow of gasoline. This is called a negative control system. Understanding this type of control system is interestingly enough something that technical people understood before biologists discovered the principle. As a rule, technology learns from biology, but as far as control systems are concerned, the process was the reverse.

Therefore when Greenpeace activists use force, for example, there occurs positive feedback: The harder you hit, the harder you will be hit back. Although it would be preferable to teach people about conservation without violence—since violence only breeds more violence—I have to admit that I am in favor of Greenpeace. I find it marvelous that these people have as much energy as they do and that they risk their lives by throwing themselves in front of tractors for the sake of conservation. If I were young, I would probably do the same thing. Now, however, my legs are too stiff, but I admire Greenpeace as such.

Nevertheless, one has to ask oneself how far these conservationists should be allowed to go. I believe that one should stop the seal hunters from hunting—for that is murder—as long as one can avoid open aggression. There are limits beyond which one should not go, however. A Greenpeace activist should not kill a seal hunter and vice versa.

However, the acts of violence perpetrated by Greenpeace conservationists are often necessary in the face of the insurmountable difficulties we find in the world. Today, it is very difficult to uncover any remnants of truly unspoiled nature, and that which remains should be defended with all vehemence. We still don't know, for example, how wild animals react when their habitat becomes too small. How small can a population be in order to survive? Is a stag still a stag when he lives in a forest enclosed by civilization? One can imagine that when an animal population and its habitat become too small, a process of domestication or inbreeding sets in and the animal is no longer what it was.

It's a similar situation to that of keeping Indians on the reservation. No one can harm them, but it's one step toward keeping them shielded in cages and in zoos. Are they then still Indians? Of course, there is still the possibility of a secondhand environment, and indeed, in a short while, we will only have such secondhand environments because the firsthand environments that we succeeded in defending are going to be more and more like small parks. As necessary as it is to maintain the firsthand environments, we still must take care to create new secondhand environments. This means farming areas where topsoil isn't blown away.

I am very satisfied to see that Tullner field is already enclosed by a border of poplars and natural brushwood. However, one could design the hedges even more ecologically so that they would benefit an enormous number of small animals and birds. One really can do a lot. A good example of a secondhand environment is the dam on the River Inn north of Passau. Night herons live there. They migrated there and didn't live there before. It is interesting that even Zarathustra knew that it was good to create secondhand environments; he considered it beneficial to transform the desert into an habitable environment. Compared with Zarathustra's transformation it is easier to gain a habitat for animals and protected areas from monoculture areas.

There is a misconception that underlies the foundation of monoculture; namely that bigger is better. I hope that this idea will soon be refuted. I must say—and it is a very responsible decision to do so—*this* ecological system no longer interests us, but *this* one is worth more than that. The last unspoiled forests, for example, don't interest us. Such a view is tremendously dangerous and can be ruinous. There is an incredible number of environments that cannot be restored if they are ruined: moors, oceans, and so on. We are obliged to defend with every means possible those environments that cannot be restored, but this does not exempt us from the duty to create secondhand environments wherever possible.

Sometimes, although much too rarely, a balance is reestablished by itself in favor of nature. Take whale hunting. Because whales have been so thinned out throughout the world's oceans, most of the world's whale fishermen have been ruined. Given those developments, it is one of my last hopes for this interesting mammal that after the very last fishing fleet has gone bankrupt, there will be one last pair of whales that will reproduce. I don't want to believe that it is too late for this kind of occurrence.

A plant that grows and blossoms at the edge of a path or in an apartment in the city can save souls. When I sit in my garden and watch the thirty-six different varieties of birds flying about uncaged there, I regain my hope and energy, and I'm happy that it's not the way it is in Wuppertal in the Ruhr region.

*A moor is probably the best example an ecological system that cannot be recreated, because a moor is created during a long evolutionary process.*

The unique symbiosis of a moor is the perfect example of a biological system that demonstrates to people that, contrary to the popular prevailing opinion, they cannot make or buy everything. In order to learn to understand the uniqueness of a moor, one must first know what moors actually are and how they appear.

Moors are, in fact, the heirs of the last ice age; that was when they began. When the glaciers retreated, they left pools of melted ice in basins that had been dug out by the glaciers and that were impermeable to water. All sorts of dead organisms accumulated in these basins. These organisms could not completely decompose or rot because the surrounding temperature was much too cold. Also, the water covering these organisms inhibited a complete decomposition.

In this way, these pools of stagnant water became increasingly filled up. Much later, plants and reeds that had taken root there also sank gradually into what once had been a pool of melted water but now was completely filled with dead organisms. Trees grew from seeds that had germinated there. However, they didn't grow tall but fell from their own weight and sank because the soft area that was drenched with water couldn't support them.

One must realize that not every swamp is a moor. The characteristic of a moor is its peat. Peat is composed of half-decomposed plants and animals—often very old organisms—that either could not rot or else could not rot completely. One can divide moors roughly into two types: The older type is the so-called upland moor. An upland moor is not one that is located on a hill but one in which rain has washed all of the nutrients to the bottom so that only very modest plants—the peat mosses or sphagnum mosses—can survive. Sphagnum moss grows over everything else, dies at the bottom, and grows upward, perhaps one millimeter a year. In unspoiled upland moors, there are cushions of sphagnum several meters thick. These are actually arched—high at the center of the moor and falling off at the edge—like an upside-down plate over the former water level of the ice-age lake. The upland moor is of inestimable value as a biological system because it takes so long to become what it is.

Then there is the low-lying bog or low moor, which arises primarily in those parts of lakes that fill up after sufficient reeds and other plants have fallen in. There are, for example, very beautiful low moors near Lake Neusiedler. A low moor is actually an unfinished moor. If one gives it enough time, one can expect that it may become an upland moor after many centuries. That is the crux of the matter! Once we have learned that our entire world requires evolutionary processes, which in the case of the moor last many thousands of years and in the case of the lowlands significantly less, then we will see that we can't be so irresponsible with these irreplaceable biological systems as we generally are. For when the last moor has been sacrificed to agriculture—in the old days to the peat cutters—then it will mean not only the extinction of a species of plant or animal—which in itself is sad because one can't recreate a species—but that of an entire biological system gone to hell.

In the upland moor, there are countless organisms that are endemic to that environment. One simply can't plop them down somewhere else. In the upland moors, for example, one finds extremely interesting meat-eating plants, such as sundew, drosera, and butterwort or the bladderwort in some pools. There are also certain rare species of birds; the golden plover, for example.

One can tell a gray heron not to sit in a meadow where trees have been cut down; to go instead to the pond, the stream, the farmer's field and gather mollusks. That's possible. Plants and animals that are found in moors are highly specialized, however; they need special ground that is poor in nutrients or oligotrophic water areas.

Moors can be replaced only by others moors. The art of creating secondhand environments doesn't help at all. Of course, one can always say that one will start a new moor. This is fine, if you can wait ten or fifteen thousand years. Then there's no problem.

Another difficulty is that the moor as an ecological system can be disturbed very easily. Even very small changes can endanger the whole system or even destroy it. You have only to spread limestone on a moor for a short time and a colossal work of nature that took ten thousand years to create is destroyed in an instant.

When the equilibrium of moors, upland moors specifically, is upset, there is practically no way to redress the situation. Even a very small loss of water is almost irreparable. I became a specialist on moors when I tried to save a moor that was endangered by a loss of water. In this instance, we had our own little upland moor near my institute at Seewiesen. Even though we immediately tried to counteract the loss of water, the birch trees spread so rapidly that they nearly supplanted all the other typical and wonderfully beautiful plants such as the sphagnum, cranberries, and buckbeans. The entire ecology changed and one couldn't do anything to prevent this from occurring. During the destruction of this moor in Seewiesen, I glimpsed one last moor frog, a male in its wedding suit, beautifully colored in shades of blue and yellow. I lived in Seewiesen for more than twenty years and went out into the moor every day, but I never saw a moor frog again. The wholesale dying had already begun. Now and then, I discovered moor lizards or adders but never a frog.

In order for a moor to survive, it must have a certain minimum size: Tiny remnants no longer constitute a moor. Moreover, a moor is not compatible with mankind and the agro-industrial needs of the farmer. One can, for example, drive cows to an Alpine pasture and let them graze for a summer. Rare orchids will grow in spite of the cows. On the other hand, it will be necessary for either the cows or the person who cuts the field to keep the grass short; otherwise, everything will become overgrown and the orchids will be quickly supplanted by other plants.

That's not possible with a moor. Moors can't tolerate even people's treading on them for a long period, because the sphagnum is so sensitive. Now, it's very difficult to convince an economically oriented person to maintain a piece of land that is useless to him, from which he can gain nothing, and on which he can't even walk. My friend Rolf Ismer, a farmer near Hannover, has a large moor. He has declared it a private nature preserve for the sake of the black grouse—black grouse especially like to live in moors. How many people would do that? This brings us back to the question of how large a moor must be in order for a species to remain there. Is Rolf Ismer's protected moor large enough to maintain the black grouse for a long time? Even animals that can adapt to small areas can suffer over the long run. One should not forget that even those creatures that possess sufficient adaptability can suffer from the small size of their habitat. They are actually more dependent on other species than one thinks. These species with which they formerly shared their habitat are dying out.

When you remove a species from a complex and interrelated biotope such as a moor, you cannot say what the effect will be on the other incredibly numerous species. Our lack of knowledge about such ecological ramifications should not be underestimated. This applies not only to moors but to all biological systems.

Of course, one can ask, "Why do I need a moor frog? To what degree is a moor frog necessary for my happiness?" Admittedly, a single species is not necessary, but the beauty of nature in equilibrium is something irreplaceable and is conducive to man's well-being—and it is that which we lose when we destroy a natural landscape like the moor.

However, as a scientist, one is confronted by one's conscience; namely, whether conservation is not, in some respects, assuming the form of a religious pseudodoctrine. One has to be very careful. The conservationist must, sooner or later, ask himself whether he should protect a habitat like the moor as it is or whether he should let things run their course? He knows that even without any such carefully directed human interference, the landscape will still change. The only thing that he should try to hinder is the effect of a rapid change caused by civilization. Take the example of the little upland moor at Seewiesen. When I notice that the moor is drier and the birch saplings are more numerous, should I go in and chop the birch trees down? Is it right to combat the birches with force so that the moor can remain a moor a little longer? In doing so, am I interfering in the course of nature and, to a certain extent, maintaining the moor in a museumlike condition? It's all too easy to create a specimen, an artificial one, for which one must constantly care.

On this particular question—whether one should passively watch while a moor dies when one could keep it alive—I am completely divided. Moors are not only beautiful and valuable because they are rare; they are also a paradigm of how easily an ecological system that is thousands of years old can be destroyed forever by one ludicrous human generation.

*In order to practice conservation effectively, one needs not only enthusiasm but also governmental support.*

It is absolutely necessary to contact sympathetic politicians if one's efforts to conserve and protect the environment are to be successful. However, one cannot expect a politician to go against his nature. Take the case of Austria's Minister for Environmental Protection. Dr. Steyrer (minister until 1986) agrees with all my proposals for effective conservation in Austria. We are of one mind, although we know that not much will be achieved, because a politician—especially a good politician who wants to aid a good cause—must act so that he will be reelected.

In the final analysis, all of the problems on earth, including conservation, are ethical problems. A democracy is unfortunately a very inappropriate climate for producing ethical results. Unethical people always receive more votes. When you come down to it, this type of government is a pitiful, unsatisfactory solution, but it is still the best of all known types of government that are at our disposal. At least in a democracy, one has the opportunity to convince many people about a given issue.

This is a fact that George Wald, the Nobel Prize winner for chemistry, discussed. Like many other scientists who turned to philosophy and especially the theory of morality in old age—industrialists would say they become diverted, whereas they are, in fact, ascending—Wald observed that the freedom of the individual—that is, true democracy—is inversely proportional to the population of a country. That means that the larger a country is, the more the population must be organized and less freedom allowed the individual.

From this, one may deduce that very large countries, aside from paying lip service to democracy, will become totalitarian. The United States and the Soviet Union provide classical examples. These are totalitarian states, and that's not good in the long run. For this reason, small countries must assume a high moral obligation. They are models and can provide more easily examples of what one should or must do.

In spite of such concerns, one discovers that the moral demands of religion are curiously and shockingly identical to those human needs that subvert conservation in favor of economic exploitation of our environment. I am an Austrian by conviction because I believe that Austria as a country has an incredibly good chance of succeeding as a democracy. Switzerland perhaps could compete with Austria as a true democracy, but there are too many rich people in Switzerland. Huge fortunes play too great a role in Swiss politics. I believe that the environmental measures that must be taken can be made popular in Austria more easily than elsewhere. I believe that the harmonization of moral and economic demands is most likely to be achieved in Austria. The demand for conservation—transmitted through the political process—is directed largely at defensive measures to preserve those beautiful, valuable, and varied natural areas that are still to be found in my country.

It appears that conservation can be successful only in wealthy countries. This means that in such countries, one at least has the possibility of instituting conservation, in contrast to poor countries whose economic situation and social structure cannot guarantee the individual sufficient nourishment or a decent standard of living. You can't, for example, convince someone in the Sahel or in a starving area of Pakistan—a person who fears for his few ears of millet and will do everything to protect them because his large and undernourished family needs every kernel of grain—that DDT is a frightful poison that is a danger to man. Nor can you forbid an Inuit, an Eskimo, to slaughter a walrus if he needs meat, oil, and bones for his immediate survival. Conservation in this sense is impossible.

Moreover, no one says that it harms nature or animals when man hunts or gathers fruit or obtains food from the soil—as long as he doesn't gain the upper hand. Primitive Indians who today still live nearly untouched in the jungles of South America have lived in harmony with nature for thousands of years despite the fact that they hunt, occasionally cultivate the soil on a small scale, and gather fruits and berries for their own needs. Nature tolerates this because the Indians interfere no more than a beast that hunts prey. When a starving individual thinks, To hell with conservation, it is because he believes that a full stomach is the most desirable thing on earth. One must understand his reasons and motivation.

Therefore, man must rise above the subsistence level in order to be receptive to conservation. This should be very possible in today's developed societies. One needs to ask oneself what one can do so that people will give the environment the attention that they should have always given it. How can one prevent mankind from committing suicide by destroying the environment so thoughtlessly as has been done up to now.

As I said, democracy is the best form of government known to teach people about conservation, but apparently it is not good enough. When I was a Russian prisoner of war, I talked with friends about the need for an institutionalization of humane legislation, and the form of government, the optimal form of government, that could best master mankind's problems. We came to the conclusion that the only efficient form of government would be a "tyranny of the good." This paradox says a lot, of course: Even if mankind was too stupid to realize that it was digging its own grave by destroying the environment, something such as an economic dictatorship would hardly be expedient. As we know, nothing is achieved by force. Every action causes a reaction, and a reign of terror would bring us back to Adolf Hitler.

Even if one had the best of intentions, a tyrannical government would end badly because every reign of terror is by definition bad. A system of government that fosters conservation and the protection of the environment and that institutes necessary measures by peaceful means has yet to be discovered. A tyranny of the good is not feasible. People have known for a long, long time, for as long as there has been human civilization, that aggression plays a significant role in politics. The demagogues knew that long before there was ethology. Hitler accused the Jews of being guilty for everything, and this propaganda had an unbelievable demagogic influence on the populace. Of course, people must be inspired to attain a common goal. One can be inspired about all sorts of things, whether they be motorcycles or science. However, it always happens that this enthusiasm is subject to certain conditions; namely, the formation of a group that has organized to support its interests. Ever since the saber-toothed tiger died out—an extinction that really threatened prehistoric man—people have lacked true enemies worth fighting. Man's framework is very adaptable: He can fight against a political opponent or a wooly mammoth. Struggle is always connected with war—it's as obvious as it is bad. Should mankind want to plunge into a world war again, then I hope for the least of all evils; namely, a world war against the destruction of the environment.

# NUCLEAR WEAPONS
## AND NUCLEAR POWER
### BEFORE AND AFTER CHERNOBYL

*W*hat is your personal opinion of nuclear weapons and nuclear power?*

There is very little that I hold in as least regard than nuclear weapons. These outgrowths of the human spirit are the most horrible thing in man's cultural development since the discovery of the hand ax, which, after all, was the beginning of everything.

As a behavioralist, I can't help arguing that human society behaves in essence like that of rats. Rats are quite peaceful— even sociable—toward members of a closed clan. However, if they encounter others of their species that belong to another "tribe," then there is murder and they turn into real devils. One could compare the situation on earth with a ship in which everything has been consumed—consumed by rats—and where aggression has increased constantly. Experience shows, however, that after such slaughter, there are usually enough rats alive to perpetuate the species. That is not so certain when men fight with nuclear weapons.

*This interview was conducted before the catastrophe at Chernobyl in April of 1986.

Some anthropologists who have researched the fossils and life of *Australopithecus,* our African ancestor, have concluded that we inherited something of the beast of prey from him, because *Australopithecus* gained his sustenance from big-game hunting, which requires brutal killing.

In reality, however, man is, as seen on the whole, a relatively harmless omnivore who couldn't defend himself particularly well from the dangers to which he was exposed. This was because he lacked special weapons such as tusks, fierce-looking claws, and the like. In contrast, real beasts of prey, such as lions and wolves, that live in packs have developed inhibitions because of their natural weapons. These inhibitions prevent their using these instruments of death against their own kind—with the exception of fights between rivals or when one pack defends itself against another. If these animals didn't have this inhibition, they would have wiped themselves out long ago.

Mankind is different: Without innate weapons, he couldn't slaughter other members of the human tribe. Lethal cases of biting and scratching were apparently rare: This would have taken too long and the afflicted would have run away. For this reason, man doesn't have any highly developed inhibitions against reciprocal manslaughter, for these inhibitions simply weren't necessary at the beginning. Then suddenly, evolution placed a stone in man's hand—the sharp, hard ax. With this new weapon, it became possible for man to kill his neighbor.

It so happens that being a human involves not only the gift of invention but also a certain degree of responsibility. Both of these characteristics are more or less in balance. The earliest man asked himself whether it was right to kill a member of the tribe with whom he got along perfectly well simply because he was in ill humor. If the human brain was not capable of posing these questions and answering them, then hominids would have died out long ago. Curiously, this sense of moral responsibility is still not a one-hundred-percent guarantee against mankind's wiping itself out. I'm thinking of nuclear weapons.

Although there has been an increase in the number of death instruments ever since the ax was invented—I also mean in the sense of complexity and technical perfection—man's inhibitions about killing have not increased apace, especially because killing has become so much easier and the man who gives the order or pushes the button is not directly confronted by the horror of his deed. Man is no longer motivated to hesitate, because now his victim is at least one hundred meters away. The initiator no longer sees the atrocity, no longer sees how the bullet tears open the abdominal wall of his enemy, a member of the same species, nevertheless, and how his intestines pour out. Perhaps this metaphor will help: Imagine that hunters are going out to hunt. All are dressed in beautiful green hunting outfits, but they have no weapons, no guns, not even bows and arrows. Then a hare appears on the scene. Which mentally sound person could force himself to kill this hare with its big eyes, long ears, and soft fur by using his fingernails or teeth?

Killing is only possible for a rational person when it is possible to separate one's feelings from all the obvious consequences. Today that's easier than before. Family men, very decent people who loved their wives and children, were still capable during the last world war of saturation bombing and gruesomely killing hundreds and even thousands of children and adults. They could do it because they were so far away. From their airplanes, these family men saw only little burning islands in the midst of a black night. This brings us to the atom bomb.

Unfortunately, I consider the collective stupidity of mankind—which is somehow incapable of learning from truly negative experiences and turning them into good—very great indeed. Still, I simply cannot believe that the superpowers would begin a nuclear war. They are too smart for this. One has to remember that if one fires, the other will fire back before one of the first two rockets has even touched the ground. Secondly, in this situation, no one will be interested any longer in conquering a certain region or territory and eliminating the people who live there, since the "victor" will not have the slightest benefit. The radiation that would be released would have a half-life of about twenty thousand years and would be dangerous, or even lethal, practically forever. One could neither breathe, drink water, or farm in a contaminated zone. I believe that this knowledge will prevent the powerful nations of this world from taking such a step—at least for a good long while—since the leaders themselves don't want to live with their children and grandchildren in fallout shelters forty meters underground. They would prefer to be in their vacation homes.

It seems to me much less likely that mankind will destroy himself with nuclear weapons than with other self-imposed catastrophes, such as pollution, overpopulation, shortsighted exploitation of fossil fuels or any other of the resources that we have on earth.

Certainly the danger is always present that an undiagnosed psychopath will gain access to the button and push it, or that a minor misunderstanding may create a state of tension and compel one superpower to an irreversible action. Such a possibility cannot be excluded. I just want to say that the potential danger of "the bomb" should be the simplest to avoid of all the dangers that threaten mankind. It's a basic fact that one has to stop making atom bombs or stop keeping them at the ready. The solution to avoiding other dangers, such as the overpopulation of our planet, is not as easy. In any event, nuclear weapons already have done a certain amount of damage by their very existence. This creates in most cognizant people a feeling of anxiety about the end of the world, an uneasiness about civilization enduring. People are forever asking themselves how long the world will continue to exist.

*Are you personally afraid of the atomic bomb?*

I am now more than eighty years old and I have had a beautiful, full life with my beloved Gretl. I know that I will certainly die during the next ten or fifteen years and yet I still rejoice as much on a sunny day as the birds that sing in my garden. I *am* afraid for my children, grandchildren, and great-grandchildren. I am more afraid of the demoralization of mankind, which could create a slow and tormented end for us all.

The cataclysm of an atom bomb would be much faster than death by demoralization, but it, too, would not be painless. It's always a question of aggression. Modern man wants to retain a "hand ax" so that he can bop his neighbor on the head when he becomes too disagreeable. Aggression is definitely an element of human behavior. If I was not at all aggressive, I would neither want to work nor be ambitious; I would neither wash nor shave. I remember that when I was a Russian prisoner of war, I lived with other doctors in a very confining shack. We had to operate all day long in an attempt to patch up mangled and torn bodies. My aggression increased tremendously due to the stress under which I was placed. One word was enough to make me throttle a good friend who was kind and decent. One evening, I went out of the hut and trampled an empty gasoline can flat—I simply needed to release pent-up tension so that I wouldn't hurt a friend because of my anger. It's always a question of cause and effect in order to master something like this.

Little children are different from adults. Watch with what abandon two- and three-year-olds pick up heavy objects with which to bop each other on the head; it's because children have no instinctive moral inhibition that prevents them from acting this way. We may be certain that this instinct was the same for the first "Cain" who killed his friend in anger with a hand ax: He didn't understand what he was doing and was certainly very stricken. The same thing can be found with higher animals.

Once upon a time, an elephant in a zoo in Munich badly hurt his keeper while he was playing, without the least intention of harming him. When the good animal realized what he had done, he became extremely agitated and stood over the keeper to protect him. This, unfortunately, prevented the keeper from receiving quick medical attention. My friend Professor Grzimek told me that a male chimpanzee in a fit of anger once bit his hand as hard as he could—chimpanzees can cause frightful wounds by biting. Only a few seconds after this fit of aggression had subsided, however, the ape tried to stanch the flow of blood by pressing Grzimek's wound together.

What I'm trying to say with these examples is this: One hopes that mankind has become clever enough to correctly assess the cause and effect of nuclear weapons so that he won't need to raise this modern hand ax against his brother in anger. It would be too late if he was sorry about it afterward. I think that my hope is not unfounded, because I know very well that aggression can be mastered more easily than other instincts, sexuality, for example. Love has certainly caused more grief in the world than murder. You don't need any special impulse to fall in love with someone—something suddenly clicks and it just happens. You can't do anything with your sense of reason to prevent the sensation.

*There is danger not only in nuclear weapons but in nuclear power. You opposed this development in the seventies and wore* NUCLEAR POWER—NO THANK YOU *badges.*

I take a very dim view of nuclear power as such. In my opinion, the danger of a catastrophe is much more imminent for the following reason: Nuclear power plants don't spring from the ground by themselves. They need a group of highly intelligent people who devise and implement them. Here we have the phenomenon whereby a group of clever gentlemen in pinstriped suits—a unified group, mind you—reject all collective guilt when something happens. They behave completely amorally and create a vehicle of danger in the world, which, if an accident occurred, could literally kill hundreds of thousands of people and cause hundreds of thousands more to die a painful death decades later as a result of the aftereffects. You find this same rejection of collective guilt with the boards of chemical firms. It's similar to a death sentence, administered by a poisonous injection: During any given experiment, there is not one executioner but three. The deadly poison is placed in only one syringe, while the other two contain a placebo. The executioners don't know, therefore, who administers the poison, and so all three feel morally guiltless.

Whoever makes atomic bombs knows that he is an instrument of death. Nuclear power plants, on the other hand, are said to be constructed for peaceful purposes, and that is precisely the snag: Those who build nuclear power plants simply don't believe that their actions are truly dangerous. They brush aside these fears and think, Nothing will happen, or, The radioactive cloud will pass over us. The truly frightening thing is that the very existence of nuclear power plants plunges humanity into a vicious cycle, because a nuclear power plant naturally gives rise to a number of energy-consuming industries. However, a nuclear power plant has a life span of only twenty-five to thirty years, and when it ceases functioning, a new one must be built.

The remains of an unused nuclear power plant continue to be dangerous—as in the case of the atomic bomb—for a half-life of twenty thousand years. This simply can't go on. I don't need any complicated economic discussions or special studies to prove that; any child who has learned about compound interest can calculate this on his fingers.

In this respect, Austria is a blessed island. I hope that all of the efforts to build a nuclear power plant here will fizzle out. I believe that in every country—except for the most primitive—there are a number of people who recognize, albeit only instinctively, the dangers that exist. Sometimes I hope that Austria—yes, humorously little Austria—will become a model in recognizing dangers. However, it may be my patriotism that causes me to have these hopes sometimes. I think that Austria acted in an exemplary manner in the case of the Hainburg nuclear power plant. Everyone believed that industry and the military would cooperate to suppress the popular referendum with force, but that didn't happen. A solution was found that was democratic in the truest and noblest sense of the word. Therefore, one can hope that the same will be true in regard to the future of other power plants, nuclear and conventional.

*What will happen in those countries that already have a number of nuclear power stations?*

That is a question that no one can answer. I don't know of any other examples during the course of my long life that would give us a clue. However, there have been small accidents that already have been mentioned in the newspapers—always very short articles printed more or less as filler. Every nuclear power plant is a highly complicated piece of equipment. Saltwater aquariums, which are also extremely complicated, break down over and over again. Just a tiny mistake, the slightest carelessness that one notices too late, can cause everything to die. I don't believe in the infallibility of the Pope, nor do I believe that the security measures at nuclear plants will someday prevent a real accident. Human nature causes us to err; it's as much a part of being human as breathing. In that respect, animals are often much more perfect in their habitat. There have been sharks and horseshoe crabs for millions of years and during this exceedingly long period of time, they have changed little or not at all because they fit into their habitat so perfectly that mutation was not necessary. Man is less perfect in what he does. The fearful danger that a nuclear power plant could break down and contaminate the water and air with radioactivity is suggested by its very existence. After all, even the crown jewels of England or priceless paintings that are guarded more carefully than nuclear power plants in the Eastern Bloc countries have been stolen despite myriad preventive measures.

*Professor Lorenz, we spoke about nuclear weapons and nuclear energy several years ago. Even then you said that you could by no means exclude the possibility of an accident involving a nuclear power plant. And now it has happened. You were right.* *

I didn't think that such an accident would happen so fast, that I would actually witness it and discuss this topic again in view of this event. As far as Chernobyl is concerned, I would like to say the following: The accident was too small. Although

*This question was raised after the accident at Chernobyl.

several dozen people lost their lives and no one knows how many will suffer from the long-term effects, the accident was too small. Of course, this sounds paradoxical and heartless toward those who suffered, and it doesn't mean that I wish, God forbid, that more people had died. I mean that the dimensions of the catastrophe were too small to be a landmark or a turning point in the thinking of those who advocate and build nuclear power plants. The best thing for humanity would have been an accident involving a nuclear power plant in which, for example, all the residents of New York City had died. Then the frightening example might have been dramatic enough to cause a rethinking. It would have been extremely lamentable and regrettable if millions of people had died as a result of a nuclear accident, but perhaps it would have been better. As it is nuclear power plants will continue to spring up like mushrooms, and even though people are talking about greater safety and increased safety measures, the danger, seen globally, will not decrease. That's why I haven't changed my opinion of nuclear energy in the least. I am certain that those responsible will continue to minimize its dangers. There will continue to be nuclear power plants.

Unfortunately, the media, which brings dreadful pictures of the devastation of Chernobyl into our homes, is powerless. On the one hand, we have the feeling that Chernobyl is so far away, while on the other, the flood of Cassandra reports from Chernobyl is too great for an individual to be able to comprehend in its entirety. The only truly effective thing we can do against radioactivity is to avoid it from the very beginning, and that requires a rethinking or reassessment of many values. The man on the street has a right to know what the mighty are doing. One has to look for concrete examples in order to make this thought comprehensible: If the ancient Egyptians, for example, had dumped radioactive fuel rods into the Nile, the river would now be contaminated and would remain so for another sixteen thousand years.

If someone doesn't understand that, then I can only say, "Father, forgive them!" and "Save our hope!"

# PART FOUR

# Man and His World

*"Man is without
a doubt
something
special. . . .
However, to say
that man is
only a mammal
from the family
of primates is
blasphemy.
Homo sapiens
are that which
is peculiar to
them, something
different from
mammals,
something much
more clever;
namely man."*

# THE YOUNG AND
# THE OLD

*S*ince time immemorial, there have been conflicts between the young and the old. How do you, Professor Lorenz, as an older person, as a scientist, and as a human being, view this universal problem?

The young and the old have always been opposed. The old have always advocated conservative principles while the young have always lobbied for the new, for growth and development. Both are necessary for the development of culture, just as genetic continuity and genetic change are indispensable for the development of a species. Without any change at all—without genetic change or without cultural revolutions—one is left with a living fossil, with a rigid system that cannot develop.

However, when the conservative element is completely lacking, one has "monsters" and "malformations." The continued existence—I don't mean vegetative but the healthy, continued existence of a species or a culture—is dependent on the existence of a healthy equilibrium between the elements of change that emanate from youth and the elements of conservatism that tend to be the province of older people. It is certainly much harder to maintain this equilibrium today than it ever was because our cultural development is accelerating exponentially, which means that the cultural distance between the generations increases with each generation. The danger that development is too rapid brings with it another very pernicious danger; namely that there is a rupture in tradition. Many young people today are not aware of how important tradition is or how much traditional knowledge is necessary for the healthy cultural and social life of a nation or a people. On the other hand, too many older people reject any change, which is equally bad. What both the young and the old least like to hear is that both are part of a so-called system of equipotential harmony that must maintain an equilibrium so that the living system—and a culture is just as much a living system as is an organism or a species—can continue to exist.

Of course, youth has a harder time today. Older people understand them less well; the enmity between the generations is very dangerous. This divergence is constantly increasing and can even lead to the downfall of our culture. Young people must bear in mind that one cannot simply "throw older people (instead of the baby) out with the bath." We don't make it very easy for the young, and I understand that the temptation to throw older people out is very great. Young people notice very quickly that today's society is not always directed and governed by the people most worthy of our confidence, because, when you come down to it, it isn't really the government that is at the helm. Rather, it is the so-called lobbies—a synthesis of money men and political men. Such lobbyists are experts, professionals of their trade and are utterly immoral.

If you take any individual executive of a multinational corporation, you will most likely find him to be a solid, decent, kind man, one whom I would immediately name the guardian of my children if I should die. When sixty of these men gather in a board of directors meeting, however, they act as though they were intellectual criminals. Each one alone is a charming old gentleman, utterly dependable, but together they plan and build factories that are extremely dangerous and harmful for the environment. Not one of these gentleman has ever committed suicide, because the individual does not feel responsible for the decisions of the group; and so it is around the world.

Now these lobbyists are, viewed collectively, not so stupid that they can't foresee the dangers of their actions, nor are they so cruel that they want to kill their own grandchildren by suffocation, poison, radioactivity, or any of the other "nice things" that we have on earth. They simply don't believe that the danger is *real*.

One way in which life is much more difficult for today's youth than for that of previous generations is that urbanization has increased so enormously. Where can one find today a child who has had as close and intensive an exposure to plants and animals in a natural garden as I did? That's why I was and am so happy! This contact was also the source of my love for animals. The fact that so many of the younger generation live in cities accounts for their blindness toward basic values.

If we ask what we can do to counteract this trend, then I am convinced that the most important solution is deurbanization. A person simply must know how beautiful a forest is, how beautiful the sea is, how beautiful every landscape that has not been spoiled by man is, how beautiful all of nature is. Children must be put in close contact with nature from their earliest years, with animals—an aquarium is a marvelous teaching tool—but, if all of that is impossible, then I believe that music provides a substitute. What is important is that people are receptive to beauty. Being receptive to the beauty of music often occurs simultaneously with an appreciation for the beauty of nature. I am convinced that one must show beautiful and venerable things to children in an effort to prevent them from having a false sense of values. Every mother can do this. She knows it from her experience as a homemaker. You can't eat paper money, and you can't spend more of your household money than you have. By this, I mean that no living system can burn up more energy than it takes in. If it does, it will die. The only legitimate source of energy on our planet is sunshine. Period. There are no counterarguments to this.

Unfortunately, most older people are not aware of this and so it becomes even more difficult, given this lack of knowledge or lack of acceptance, to transmit such knowledge to one's own children. A cogent example should be fossil fuel, which we use in a ruinously fast and loose way. It's so simple that every elementary school child should be able to understand. Natural gas, oil, and coal are nothing other than the remains of prehistoric forests that arose because of the sun's nourishment and that geologic processes put under the surface of the earth. The affluent societies of Europe and America today are involved in the shortsighted process of exploiting these reserves in order to achieve great profits. However, how long will this continue? I am completely convinced that the multinational corporations that, together with their extremely clever technical engineers, devise the most lucrative methods of exploitation—by this I mean mining—do not lose any sleep over the fact that their "capital," which has been dormant under the earth for millions of years, will one day be used up. Let's ignore the question of harm to the environment. What are these engineers going to use to heat the planet when there are no more fossil fuels? Their paper money?

One can demonstrate easily that anyone who is blind to genuine values spent his childhood far removed from nature. Whoever has gone snorkeling near a coral reef or hunting in an unspoiled forest can no longer be a slave to money or blind to genuine values.

The big difference between the past and the present is that most cultures today have largely lost their autonomy. If blacks, Japanese, and Indians did not have their own characteristic skin color and appearance, they would, insofar as they live in big cities, be interchangeable. Habits of dress and manners are becoming more and more similar on all continents. This has a particular influence on youth. Never before was the youth of all races so similar as today. Computer games, T-shirts, television, and pop music are international. Never before has youth distanced itself so quickly and so internationally from older folk, people who are still rooted in tradition. That frightens me a bit.

Nonetheless, it is a normal process for young people to separate themselves from older people. Scientists realize that this process is, among others things, motivated by aggression. I know this from my own observations when I had an institute in Seewiesen. All the young people in our group had long hair and unkempt beards, went barefoot, and wore blue jeans from head to toe. This behavior went on for quite a while. Suddenly, one day, I caught myself in the act of dressing up in a suit and tie for my seminar. I was, so to speak, donning war clothes and putting on war paint. I was embarrassed and took them off, however. It's the same as when two rival Indian tribes face each other threateningly, each in its particular regalia. In other words, today's youth distances itself from older people as though they were two distinct ethnic groups. This lack of understanding of one another—of which clothes is only one manifestation—leads to an ever-quickening avalanche of mutual estrangement, which is very dangerous.

This tendency is increased by the fact that all young people are particularly susceptible and receptive to demagogues. It's natural when young people are in the process of leaving their parents. One wants to be different, no matter what it costs, from one's father with his daily ritual of breakfast, office, and evening relaxation in front of the television.

In this phase of their development, young people have an extreme tendency—I would say almost an addiction—to join a group that is completely different from what they have. If such a group doesn't exist, they make one. The group's goal is, ultimately, to be independent and to oppose other groups— if necessary even to oppose God and the entire world. That's why propagandists, demagogues, and all sorts of sectarians can win young people over very easily.

Another aspect is that, strangely enough, most children react negatively to being spoiled in comfortable middle-class homes. Young people understand very quickly that their parents' unlimited belief in economic growth and love of money is false and fruitless. This understanding can lead some young people to despair or even ruin. What they lack are the right models. The father is no longer a model. He may suffer from ulcers caused by the stress of his job, and he doesn't have the time to deal sympathetically with his son and daughter, anyway. Young people do not find models in government anymore, either. Democracy functions very poorly, although I realize that it is still the best form of government we have.

Aldous Huxley once offered his own version of the Roman "bread and circuses" by saying: Give me hamburgers, cola, and television and for God's sake spare me all the talk about responsibility and freedom! Because of the high level of affluence in today's society, young people are simply oversatiated. This leads in every respect to indolence. Such pathological boredom on the part of young people during puberty can lead to serious depressions and even suicide. This fact can be proven scientifically. Yet, as macabre as it may seem, an unsuccessful suicide can, in a certain sense, do some good. A man whom I know instructs the blind. He told me that he teaches young people who had attempted suicide by shooting themselves in the head; the bullet severed the nerves that control their sense of sight but didn't kill them. None of these young people ever made another attempt to take their "ruined" life; on the contrary, they were much more balanced and adjusted than they had been when in full possession of their physical faculties. From this lesson, one may infer that people who are deathly bored due to the lack of positive models in their life need a difficult barrier to overcome in order to find meaning in their lives.

Our ancestors faced many difficult problems in their daily lives. Their existence was more balanced than our own, for they encountered a combination of painful and pleasurable experiences. *Both* sensations were matters of immediate concern. Anyone, for example, who has really suffered from hunger—I was a Russian POW and so I think I can speak from experience—knows what a divine gift it is to have unlimited nourishment.

Wild animals still live in this way. In order to catch its prey, an animal on the prowl must do certain things that it would rather not. It must run through deep snow or jump into icy water, and much more. If it were well fed, it would hardly do such things voluntarily with such intensity. The animal is driven, to do these unpleasant things by hunger, but the animal reckons that effort and result must be in equilibrium. A barn owl cannot afford to do a slipshod job of hunting mice during a frosty winter. Its efforts are carefully calculated and must be directed toward a goal. If the owl merely flew about aimlessly, it would consume more energy that it could replace by the food it caught, with the result that it would finally fall exhausted from the gable.

Our ancestors spent almost all of their time looking for food and had to weigh whether certain efforts and hikes would be rewarded with a full stomach. During these earlier periods, it was by no means a sin to stuff oneself until one burst, since one didn't know when one would eat again. Much of what we consider a vice today was a virtue then, essential for survival— cowardice, for example. However, even the earliest philosophers knew, since mankind by then already lived much better, that it was *not* desirable to avoid everything unpleasant. It was necessary to take the good with the bad. Today, technical progress provides us with shortcuts in almost every area, and therefore we have become effeminate, indolent slaves of comfort, people who are weary of life; this then weighs, in particular, on the collective spirit of the young people.

# · OVERPOPULATION ·

*P*  *eople require more and more room to live, which reduces the space left for nature. Isn't this development leading our species into a dead end?*

A Turkish friend of mine who is oddly enough a professor of economics in San Francisco once formulated the following terse dictum: All of the dangers that threaten mankind today result, in the final analysis, from overpopulation. None of them can be solved by any method other than education.

I agree with him unconditionally. These are irrefutable facts.

However, how we solve this disastrous overpopulation is a problem that has no solutions so far. It is certainly one of the most difficult problems facing mankind today because it involves so many ethical issues.

That exponential growth in finite space must lead sooner or later to catastrophe is as clear to me as it is to every child. The big question is *when* will we reach the end? This is impossible to answer, we can say only that there is a limit.

Of course, one tries to find countervailing measures, but these solutions not only seem ineffective but indeed are. The same situation holds true for medicine. For quite some time, medicine has been able to recognize the causes of diseases but has been unable to eliminate the diseases themselves. People are helpless when a new virus appears. At present, I believe that AIDS is truly dangerous as far as the future is concerned. Perhaps AIDS will become the Black Plague of our century and of the next. No one knows. Or perhaps it will be another disease that reduces the population everywhere in the world. However, one should neither hope nor expect that something like this will help to stem the tide of overpopulation.

In connection with the problem of overpopulation, I was asked by journalists whether or not the human race will behave like lemmings. I always used to answer, "No, not at all, because lemmings migrate when it is necessary, when they have multiplied too much. In contrast to people, lemmings don't decimate the area in which they live. That's a big difference!

In general, animals can provide good examples of how one can counteract the catastrophe of overpopulation. Just limiting an animal's territory brings about a certain natural control of the population, and frequently animals will not mate unless they have found an appropriate territory. If one takes rabbits as an example, one sees that these animals have developed such strong mechanisms to inhibit their own reproduction that a rabbit embryo that is already growing will atrophy if there is an overpopulation of rabbits in the territory. There is a direct interaction between rabbits and their mortal enemies, wolves. When there is an overpopulation of rabbits, then the wolves in the area don't form packs, with the result that all the she-wolves become highly fecund and bear lots of young because there is food for all of them. When rabbits are scarce, wolves form packs because they must attack larger prey such as elks. Then, because wolves have a highly complex social structure in the pack environment, only one she-wolf assumes the role of the head of the pack. Only she is impregnated, so that there is only one litter per year. A natural process of birth control exists and therefore none of the animals goes hungry or dies of starvation.

150

*This brings us to the question of whether birth control among people is appropriate for controlling overpopulation.*

This question leads us to an impasse. The issue concerns me a great deal but remains somehow an insoluble dilemma. If you look at the situation, you will discover that everything that human nature prescribes in this respect militates against birth control. The highest principle of the doctor and science as a whole is to save the life of a premature baby with any means available. Similarly, it is certainly unethical to destroy the lives of unborn children by abortion. It's not just an embryo in a body, from the very first second, it is a human being, although not completely developed. Nevertheless, the solution is birth control, but only on a theoretical level, because this is not morally justifiable. If a government in power should proscribe birth control by law, then that would be a horrid authoritarian use of power. Such a law would bring us very close to the horrible events that occurred during the dictatorship of Adolf Hitler.

In the face of these gigantic problems, one naturally remains a prisoner of the system of values derived from one's family and the culture from which one has emerged. Even my father, who was fifty-five years older than I, was completely convinced that the good that medicine does for the individual is bad for the species as a whole. When a doctor, nurse, or Peace Corps volunteer arrives in a tropical land, he or she can't help but lower the infant mortality rate, if only for the sake of human decency. When you see children with huge stomachs bloated by hunger—their bodies like skeletons covered with skin, racked by hellish diseases and eye infections—then you invariably give them the last piece of bread you have in your lunch bag. When I as a doctor enter a village of Indians or African natives, I do the same, because it would be tantamount to suicide if I didn't. If one goes against one's own moral requirements, one harms oneself to such an extent that one perishes. In other words, it is suicide for a doctor not to help a sick person, even though one is doing the worst harm to a primitive tribe by reducing its infant mortality. In arid areas where people have lived for thousands of years and wrested meager nourishment from the poor soil, it's completely natural that infant and child mortality rates be enormously high by our standards. If one preserves the lives of too many children, then one increases the suffering of the entire population of the village because the soil and water supply are overtaxed and cannot support more people than are already there. Such people have managed very well without us for centuries, but once we have begun in good faith to "help" them, then for moral reasons there is no turning back. It's a vicious circle.

This brings us to the religious aspect. Here I cannot help but say that I am torn. I am not a Christian, but I affirm all of the moral demands of Christianity. To this extent then, I am a Christian. I don't feel any resentment or animosity toward Christianity because I grew up in two families that lived according to its precepts—although no one believed in life after death. I'm speaking of my parents and my wife's parents.

I don't believe that the Pope is infallible. I believe that he's a decent person and that he wants to do good. He feels obliged for ethical reasons and for the sake of the church to preach against contraception, including the Third World. I believe that he knows very well that he's playing into the devil's hands, and that this realization weighs on him. By his indirect demand that the poorest of the poor should bring an unlimited number of children into the world, the Pope has ruined the lives of many of my personal friends who were sympathetic toward Christianity. Who will feed these children? I think of the missionaries who have traveled to the farthest corners of the earth to save souls. They are extremely decent people. You need to meet one of these missionaries to understand what admirable, idealistic, and kind people they are. Yet these people have done the worst thing that one can do to primitive people. Missionaries are not guiltless in regard to the fact that the natives of Papua are now uprooted from their culture, deracinated from the religion of nature that had kept them alive for thousands of years. They now wear T-shirts with Coca-Cola signs printed on them and carry portable radios instead of bows and arrows. A true compromise between the moral imperative and the demands of science has yet to be found.

However, no philosopher's precept has yet to be discovered that could determine what one can actually *do* to effectively counteract our exponential population explosion. We have not found a solution that would not violate the valuable moral and ethical beliefs that distinguish man as man.

It's easier with animals. There is what one might call a natural homosexuality in the animal kingdom. If you put two doves in a cage, they will mate immediately. They make a nest and only when they see that no eggs are laid do they realize that they are two females. It happens occasionally that two male dogs meet on the street and will mount one another as a substitute. Now and then, one observes a very pronounced homosexuality in geese. Two males become friends and live as a couple. They perform all of the rites of living together and are sometimes faithful to one another for ten years. One encounters the same phenomenon among many different species in thousands of different forms. Naturally, we should welcome everything that counteracts overpopulation, but homosexuality is, needless to say, no solution for mankind. Everything that concerns the "highest mammal"—man—is much more difficult because man is a cultural being.

When viewed alone, evolutionary escalation is a positive kind of feedback. Every type of growth becomes stronger as it progresses. An organic being draws energy to itself, grows, and in this growing accumulates greater and greater energy. That this kind of growth only rarely leads to a catastrophe, that such overgrowth is an exception, is explained by the fact that certain inorganic powers keep all forms of life within bounds.

A sapling, for example, doesn't grow in a linear manner, one through twenty-three, but two, four, eight, sixteen, because it grows on all sides. It grows roughly conically, and conical growth can only last for a certain time. There is an old saying, "No tree grows to heaven." Therein lies a very deep truth. There is always a mechanism that ensures that a tree that has grown too tall will topple. This equilibrium is especially important. The mouse is dependent on the weasel that eats it, because without the weasel, the mouse would perish from an overpopulation of mice. However, it isn't good if there are too many weasels either, because there wouldn't be enough mice for food. Therefore, an equilibrium between two species that are dependent on one another is the most desirable system. Under this precondition, the system can continue to function for a long, long time. That's true of the mouse and the weasel and of a tree that is hindered from growing too tall by its inner construction, which will support only a certain level of stress.

However, we now come to the big exception: No natural law prevents an industrial enterprise from becoming too big, powerful, and grasping. An industrial enterprise *can* grow up to heaven! That is one of the biggest dangers facing humanity. Karl Marx was entirely right when he said that the larger enterprises devour the smaller ones, thereby condemning the craftsman to extinction. A cobbler cannot prevail against a shoe factory; he will inevitably go bankrupt. All escalating forces—and that's especially true for the economy—are usually fatal. Every pair of opponents, whether they be shoe manufacturers or toy manufacturers, will compete until they harm one another.

Now this mutual battle to the death is also observed in the animal kingdom; for example, by rival members of the same sex. In many species, this rivalry ends without bloodshed, but with certain types of apes, the new head of the band or pack kills all of the offspring of its predecessor solely for the purpose of creating room for its own offspring. It's the same with lions. A new pasha kills all newborns so that the she-lions will be ready sooner to be impregnated by him. That sounds horrid, but there is a certain sense to a process that strikes us as so awful. The stronger and faster simply prevail, and this, in turn, helps the species to remain healthy.

The trouble is that this isn't true of the rivalry between industrial enterprises. When one multinational corporation subdues another, this is not necessarily better; one can't say that in doing so it improved its nature and benefited the human species.

*Weren't new and unspoiled tracts of land also first conquered by certain industrial conglomerates?*

That's very true, but people think about this much too little; they overlook this knowledge even though it's an important factor.

The first people who forged their way into the jungles of our world were greedy people who took gold from the Indians. Shortly thereafter came missionaries and explorers. However, this intrusion only became really pernicious when man had the technical means to leave enduring marks in these remote regions of the earth. The best, or rather the worst, example is provided by the processors of luxury woods in Europe as well as in Japan and elsewhere. They were the first to cut gigantic paths in the primeval forests so that they could move their equipment to the spot where they were working. One can't say that they totally destroyed the forest, since they only took trees that were of a certain minimum size and therefore worth the effort. However, when a huge tree is felled, it naturally knocks down countless other trees and saplings. Nevertheless, I think that the primeval forest could have survived that.

That which followed was much worse, however. Because of the newly created paths for transportation, it was possible for poor, starving farmers to advance deeper and deeper into the forest. It is these farmers who, to a great degree, finish off the forest: All of the trees and plants are cut down and then burned. It's a great mistake to think that the forest floor is rich in nourishing material; it thrives, so to speak, on itself, since the leaves that fall to the forest floor are immediately recycled into food for living organisms. It's an almost perfect cycle, but the forest floor has practically no reserves. The farmers are well aware of this, which is why they burn the trees. This fertilizes the ground for a short while, perhaps for three or four harvests. Then, however, the area is ecologically decimated and the farmer has to look for new land and again slash and burn. Therefore, the poorest of the poor just barely survive and produce a great number of descendants who must be fed.

Once the farmer departs, the forest floor is destroyed forever. A little bit of grass grows for a while and *then industry returns again.* I recently heard that automobile companies provide money for clearing and developing forests. When the soil turns to steppe and only grass can grow, then the cattle ranchers from North America appear and drive their gigantic herds across the poor soil where a thick forest once proliferated. Supposedly big ranching firms—companies that raise cattle for meat—are behind the destruction of the forest in Paraguay. That's a crime against humanity. The shortsightedness leading to the destruction of the equatorial jungles is so immoral that it could have been inspired by Satan himself. There are many reasons, such as overpopulation, for opposing this destruction of the jungles. The multinational corporations promote so-called progress by encouraging settlers to advance on the roads that the conglomerates build into the most remote corners of the earth. They also contaminate the cultures of these so-called primitive people—people who have had natural birth control for thousands of years in the form of a high child-mortality rate. By forcing Western Culture upon these people or simply by robbing the wild tribes of their habitat by clearing the jungle, they bring about catastrophic destruction.

I'd like to see what would happen if a cattle rancher who clears jungles suddenly came home to his villa and found strange people digging up his garden, chopping down his palm trees, and carrying away the roof of his house. That's exactly how the Stone Age people must feel when we clear the jungle where they previously lived in complete harmony, never having taken more from their environment than any other carnivore or plant eater. In addition to all the evils that I have just enumerated, I'd like to add the irrefutable fact that the jungles are sensitive regulators of our climate and they influence the weather and seasons all around the world. Moreover, a significant portion of the oxygen that we breathe comes from the photosynthesis of the jungle, in addition to that of the algae in the sea.

*We now see the effects of overpopulation not only in relatively remote parts of the earth but also in civilized countries and in the concentrated areas of the big cities.*

That is, of course, a phenomenon that has occupied me for a long time. This extremely peculiar overpopulation in the big cities has caused an complete loss of human warmth, which, I would maintain, has reached pathological proportions. Perhaps one realizes how hospitable people can be when one occasionally visits a chalet in the mountains. Although one is a stranger, one is offered food, drink, and a place to sleep as a matter of course. Just try that in a big city! If one enters an apartment where people don't know one, they'll quickly call the police.

I once had an unforgettable experience that was quite similar. My wife and I were entertaining a couple from Wisconsin who were professional conservationists. They had spent an entire year in a little house in the wilderness, completely cut off from everything else. One evening, when it was time for supper, we heard the shrill sound of the doorbell just as we were sitting down at the table. Somewhat uncontrolled, I said, "For God's sake, who can that be?" This utterance shocked my guests more than if I had asked them to eat out of the dog's bowl. For this couple who had just spent the entire year in the wilderness, it was entirely incomprehensible that one wouldn't react with pleasure to an unexpected knock at the door.

This kind of slight unfriendliness, which escalates to an unmanageable level in large, overpopulated cities, is the beginning of inhumanity. Man apparently was not created so that he could live successfully crammed together for a long time. He begins to lose his sense of empathy and becomes aggressive. This tendency is especially pronounced in the large cities of North America where groups of young people gather together and in one night slash a hundred car tires or break windows in a completely senseless way in order to release their pent-up aggression. Such behavior is certainly attributable to the curse of overpopulation.

I have yet another thought on this matter. A second curse that weighs heavily on overpopulated, civilized countries is the degree of comfort found there. The fact that people are so accustomed to comfort makes a regression almost impossible. Man doesn't want to renounce the comforts that he enjoys. The pioneers knew one or two hundred years ago when they gave the Indians firewater that they would make these primitive people dependent on new pleasures. Today, we have made ourselves to a very high degree slaves to comfort.

Modern man in civilized countries has woven a tapestry of fatal dependencies that drive him into a position of total subjugation. Who is ready to dispense with central heating and electricity? When the boiler breaks down in my house and I have to shave with cold water, I am not delighted, even though I know that one could live without the comfort of hot water. Once there was a total blackout in New York City and the resulting chaos was astounding; most people thought that the end of the world had come.*

To forfeit these comforts in civilized countries is, I believe, one of society's greatest problems. Naturally, the increase in economic and industrial growth in the Western world can also lead to real catastrophes. That's why a period of no economic growth should not only be a theoretical possibility but also a pressing demand. One continually has to remind all unconditional advocates of forced economic development that such catastrophes loom.

If we don't succeed in stemming the tide of overpopulation and of all those dangers that result from it, then we will be in a truly untenable situation.

My friend Otto Koenig once offered a marvelous example of the contradictory way in which man behaves in the world. He said, "Man behaves on earth as does a rabbit in Australia."

*Trans. note: There were, in fact, two total blackouts in New York City, one in 1965 and the other in 1977.*

This means that man in his pernicious way doesn't really belong in this otherwise harmonious world and that his inability to belong or blend in destroys everything around him. Likewise, rabbits don't belong in Australia; they were taken there and in a short time they multiplied so quickly that they transformed an entire countryside of usable soil into a wasteland. If we want to overcome the dangers that threaten us—overpopulation being among the greatest—then we must radically change our way of thinking. We must reassess all of our values and diminish the esteem in which we hold money. There is room for optimism: Among those who are not yet twenty-five, there is hardly anyone who venerates money. However, among people who are about forty, you will find many who do, and among those who are about sixty, very many. Youth is our greatest source of hope.

# THE FUTURE:
# A WORLD
# WITHOUT MAN?

*W*hen one thinks of all the dangers that threaten us—
*radioactivity, the destruction of forests and waters, and
so on—then this question arises: Will there be a final
apocalypse? Will the future be a world without man?*

All of the dangers that we have mentioned grow more threatening and more burdensome from year to year. There remains
only the hope that man will understand in time that counter-
measures must be found that are morally justifiable on the one
hand and on the other effective enough to save the world. This
will be very difficult. One needs not only people who can warn
but those who can act; that is, politicians.

One only requires good common sense to recognize all of
the dangers, but I believe that many people today have lost
their common sense. Man has fallen into an inner mental con-
flict and believes that the real world lacks any true values. *This
is an error;* every person whose eyes are open knows this to be
the case. This sense of values is a trait that must be regarded
as common to all men. Whosoever was trained with a correct
perception of shape—Gestalt—must find the biological world

beautiful and must regard its beauty optimistically; and whoever has these values feels empathy for every creature and every natural system. Even scientists are not immune to these emotions—in a positive sense. An incident in Charles Darwin's life illustrates this. During one of his great expeditions, he accidentally discovered an unknown species of spider. The spider had just caught an insect in its web. What did he do? Instead of watching the insect die, which must have interested him from a scientific view, he intervened and freed it.

However, all of these noble traits of man are subject to certain inhibitions—the rejection of collective guilt, for example. It's an extremely dangerous symptom that people willingly shrug off responsibility. It happens when an intelligent man is inducted into the army. He knows what is happening, but he simply can say, "I'm not responsible," even if a war was to break out. It's the same when a worker in South America sets his chain saw to a huge tree in the jungle. He says, "I'm not responsible, I'm only doing my job."

A newspaperman once asked me in connection with this concept why we simply don't let people continue to live as long as possible and when man dies out, just accept a world without people. To that, I can say that plants and animals have always died out in the course of the development of the earth. However, the species did not disappear forever but was replaced by others that were better adapted to changes in the environment. For example, a change in the environment—a natural change—is responsible for the fact that there is desert in many regions where several thousand centuries ago there was green land and a great variety of plants and animals. Even the hottest desert isn't dead, however. There are indeed organisms that have adapted to these extreme conditions and are viable.

The same principle holds true with civilizations. When a European goes to the Kalahari, he won't survive for two days unless he has brought enough food and water with him. The bushmen who have been living there for many thousands of years have learned to adapt. There is practically no rainfall and yet they find enough liquids in various plants to stay alive.

When the Spanish under Cortez arrived to subjugate the so-called wild people and to take their gold, many white men died not only of tropical diseases but also from eating wild fruits, because they didn't know what was edible and what was toxic. An Indian knows this very well because he has *adapted* to his environment since time immemorial. What I'm trying to say is that adaptation is always an evolutionary process, and evolution requires time. Darwin discovered that, among other things, and we have apparently forgotten it again. There is indeed a vast difference between man dying out on his own and man eradicating himself.

Man is in essence just one species among many, and at present the "highest," but his situation is very precarious because he has become too clever. He has become so clever that he sufficiently comprehends the natural preconditions of his life in order to destroy them, but he is not smart enough to maintain these natural preconditions. If things continue as they have, man will not die out—which he must do sooner or later, in any case—but he inevitably will destroy himself through a radioactive holocaust, a total pollution of the environment, or something equally lethal. That is the essence of his irresponsibility. If mankind alone dies out, then that is the end of the highest form of life. If one doesn't see any value in man, then one can say that is all right and can accept that now another form of life can come—one that will probably have a similar process of development and will become the highest form of life. That's definitely possible. A few thousand centuries ago, there was a world with countless plants and animals and no man, and the planet functioned faultlessly, *even better than with people.* The larger danger, however, is that our species will *wipe itself out* and pull everything else organic with it to its final destruction. That is truly unethical.

Man is without a doubt something special. Of course, man always needs structure, and one can say that Homo sapiens are mammals from the family of primates. That is unquestionably true. However, to say that man is *only* a mammal from the family of primates is blasphemy. Homo sapiens are that which is peculiar to them, something different from mammals, something much more clever; namely, man. That's why it would be such a loss if man was to disappear. Man is not man when he's alone; he is per force a member of society. That is true to a slight degree of chimpanzees, is definitely true of geese, and is not true of mussels.

There are a lot of my contemporaries who adhere with almost religious faith to the belief that nothing can happen to man. They believe that through science and technology we can build a kind of protective shield that will keep us alive forever. No one knows. Perhaps a vision of the future will materialize: a world where we will all live in cities, swallow artificial food pills, and run about with oxygen masks. Perhaps that would be technically feasible. However, if that should come to pass, then man would still be ruined, because all of the civilized relations that hold people together would come to a halt and there would be an end to our feelings, which is exactly what distinguishes us. A decrease in these traits would have an equally tragic effect on the harmonious world in which we live. Man has to remember that more than ninety percent of all people up until now were hunters and gatherers; only the remainder farmed and kept livestock. Only a very small percentage devoted themselves to industry. For that reason, the genetic matter that has been handed down to us is hardly different from that of Stone Age men. However, man's cultural development has been much more rapid than his biological development. Today's modern culture entices him to commit great mistakes.

This can be seen in the case of advertising. When animals court or "advertise," when a bird puffs up its crop to impress a female, it does it for itself and for the benefit of the species. The bird that puffs up its crop the best and has the finest crop obtains the desired mate. This process of selection ensures that the strongest can continue to reproduce and maintain the health of the species.

Man also courts or advertises. I feel obliged as a scientist to advertise, to sit here and advertise for a good cause, just as I feel obliged to transmit my own knowledge to my students. The expectation linked with this type of "courting" is that of truthfulness; in particular, convincing others with arguments. Advertising today, however, takes a completely different route. Primarily, there is no longer just the transmission of the fact that a certain product exists; instead, the feelings of the potential buyer are stimulated. One could say that with scientific methods advertising experts have discovered that simply transmitting facts is not advantageous; one must address the deeper layers of the human consciousness if one is to be successful. Then one can easily manipulate people. Advertisements for racy sports cars make the buyer think that he will be as handsome and successful as the driver of the car in the ad.

In many areas, people preach a paradise on earth. The media provides us with rose-colored glasses, and that is immoral and very bad. Take for an example the family epics on television: On these shows, the forests aren't dying; the world is all right. Advertising shows us a world intact, and we believe it. I admit that I, too, watch such programs, but only when I am very tired and haven't anything better to do. It is, of course, relaxing in a certain sense to know in advance that the bad guys always get what they deserve. That's why I read Tolkien, who uses the same devilish and seductive methods. However, most people probably find it very difficult to return to the real world after they have been influenced by advertising every day on the radio and on television.

This leads to a great danger, which one can describe as "inability to bear discomfort." Hardly anyone today wants to invest hard work into achieving a goal merely for the joy of anticipation and the true satisfaction at the end. In practically everything, people seek immediate satisfaction. Modern life makes instant gratification very attainable. That one becomes a frightful slave to money in doing so is hardly clear to anyone.

My teacher Oskar Heinroth said, *"Homo homini lupus"*: man is the wolf of man. There is a deep truth in this. In the old days, the saber-toothed tiger and the cave bear exercised a certain process of selection on man; today, that process is exercised by man on man in a constant battle for success and financial power. This situation is much more dangerous, because all of the values that *cannot be bought* become unimportant. For that reason, it is possible that mankind will die a slow and painful death in the near future because of demoralization.

However, I am an optimist. I know from animals that lying to oneself in advertising doesn't pay. Perhaps it's my optimism that allows me to believe that even the media has improved a little. Mankind must learn a lot, however, and the frightening thing about this is that we must learn fast. The past suggests that this won't happen, because the masses are lazy. If one projects the world's situation into the future, then anything could happen. If we don't stop the deterioration of the forests in Europe, then we can be reasonably certain that huge areas will turn to steppe. If we destroy the jungle, it won't grow back. Parts of it are being destroyed right now, areas as large as West Germany every year. With the destruction of the jungle will come a change in the climate: The glaciers on the Poles will partially melt and this will lead to devastating floods. If we destroy the oceans, then organisms that are vital for our survival will die, and the algae that provide us with oxygen will also die.

One could enumerate this Cassandra prophecy further and discuss details. The future looms as a colorful mosaic of dangers and we cannot ignore it as we are doing now. Politicians, the mighty of the world, should stop wearing blinders. It is their job to take action. When a person is taken to the hospital with a ruptured appendix, the doctor cannot say, "We'll have to think about it and reach an agreement about what to do. We'll wait until next week or next month." By that time, the patient would be dead. It is the same with the threats to all of humanity: They will prove fatal if we wait too long.

A friend of mine who was a pious Quaker once said, "Religiosity is the realization of belonging to a community, in complete responsibility, which is much nobler than the individual, than oneself." I hope that this feeling of personal responsibility can be transferred to the ecological totality of our world, even if the individual doesn't know what biology is.